MANAGING IN A BUSINESS CONTEXT

CIPD REVISION GUIDE

STEPHEN TAYLOR

Chartered Institute of Personnel and Development

Published by the Chartered Institute of Personnel and Development,
CIPD House, Camp Road, London, SW19 4UX

First published 2003

Design by Pumpkin House, Cambridge

Typeset by Pumpkin House, Cambridge

Printed in Great Britain by The Cromwell Press, Trowbridge, Wiltshire

British Library Cataloguing in Publication Data
A catalogue of this manual is available from the British Library

ISBN 1 84398 021 5

The views expressed in this manual are the author's own and may not necessarily reflect those of the CIPD.

The CIPD has made every effort to trace and acknowledge copyright holders. If any source has been overlooked, CIPD Enterprises would be pleased to redress this for future editions.

Chartered Institute of Personnel and Development,
CIPD House, Camp Road, London, SW19 4UX

Tel: 020 8971 9000   Fax: 020 8263 3333

Email: cipd@cipd.co.uk   Website: www.cipd.co.uk

Incorporated by Royal Charter   Registered Charity No. 1079797

MANAGING IN A BUSINESS CONTEXT

CIPD REVISION GUIDE

Stephen Taylor is the CIPD Associate Examiner for Managing in a Business Context. He is also a senior lecturer in human resource management at Manchester Metropolitan University. He is a leading academic and writer in the field.

The Chartered Institute of Personnel and Development is the leading publisher of books and reports for personnel and training professionals, students, and all those concerned with the effective management and development of people at work. For details of all our titles, please contact the publishing department:

tel: 020-8263 3387

fax: 020-8263 3850

e-mail: publish@cipd.co.uk

The catalogue of all CIPD titles can be viewed on all the CIPD website:

www.cipd.co.uk/bookstore

CONTENTS

Contents

• PREFACE

The CIPD's Managing in a Business Context paper is tough to prepare for because of the wide range of very diverse topic areas that are covered by its standards. Some relate to developments in the business environment specifically (political, legal, technological etc), while others focus on ways in which organisations interact with their specific business environments (eg; strategy-making and ethical considerations). The standards encompass detailed issues that relate to the UK or to particular industries as well as bigger and more controversial global trends. As a result examination questions can be asked that require candidates to write about their own organisations, their industrial sector, their region, the country as a whole, Europe or indeed the world. It is a very broad field and thus hard to revise effectively.

This book has been written to help you prepare more thoroughly and, in particular, to help you use the time you have available for study more effectively. Specifically, it contains sections which cover the following:

i) a reminder of the CIPD's standards in Managing in a Business Context. This should help you to plan your study and revision profitably

ii) guidance on the shift from PQS (the professional qualification scheme) to the PDS (professional development scheme) and what this means for the design of exam papers and questions

iii) information about what we examiners are looking for when marking your Managing in a Business Context papers

iv) a section setting out the common reasons that candidates have for performing poorly or failing the Managing in a Business Context examination

v) a section setting out the most common reasons for the awarding of high marks in the Managing in a Business Context examination

vi) two practice papers for you to use when revising

vii) full feedback to all the questions on both these papers.

Why, a portion of candidates ask, is it necessary for prospective HR professionals to demonstrate such a wide range of knowledge about aspects of the business environment? Why, for example, are we required to know about the legal system, EU initiatives, world economic institutions or technological developments that have little or nothing in themselves to do with the management of people? Why do we need to know about trends that have no great relevance for our organisations? These are good questions. To understand the answers you need to appreciate the purpose of the CIPD's membership requirements.

First it is necessary that people entering and representing the HR profession have credibility with other managers and with members of other professional groups. Historically a major complaint of personnel professionals was that they were not listened to by managers in other disciplines, that they lacked authority and were not taken seriously when decisions were being taken. One of the reasons for this was an inability on the part of personnel specialists to contribute to discussions outside their particular range of professional expertise. They were listened to when giving advice about dismissals or performance-management, but not even asked when it came to wider strategic decision-making in the organisation. As a result our profession has tended to be seen as a poor relative of other more significant management disciplines and relatively few HR specialists have been in a position to succeed to senior general management roles. The Managing in a Business Context paper helps to ensure that those now entering the profession do not suffer from this historic lack of credibility, that they are able to speak with authority about the major debates of our time and contribute effectively to thinking within organisations about long term responses to environmental trends.

Secondly, it is important to remember that in sitting the CIPD's exams you are seeking membership of a profession whose members work across all the industrial sectors. You may work in the public sector now, but your CIPD membership will assist you to move into other areas. In five year's time you may be working for an international company operating in a wholly different industrial sector (or vice versa). The Managing in a Business Context standards aim to provide you with a foundation of knowledge and understanding about developments in the business world that span well beyond your current daily concerns. This is necessary in order to facilitate any future move you may be interested in across to a wholly different type of organisation.

Thirdly, as a member of the CIPD you should be able to make a very real contribution to wider debates that have relevance for the management of people in organisations. You need to know about long term social and demographic trends because these effect your labour markets. You need to know how the legal system works because it produces and interprets law in ways that have direct relevance to the way people are managed. The same is true of European matters, technological developments and longer term economic and political trends. All these matters impact or have the potential to impact on your core HRM activities. Studying the Managing in a Business Context standards allows you to understand both the 'what' and the 'why' when it comes to significant environmental developments. Gaining this understanding enhances your professional standing, increases your credibility and thus helps give you sufficient influence to make a real proactive contribution to decision-making your organisation.

● GENERAL EXAMINATION GUIDANCE

The CIPD launched its new Professional Development Scheme (PDS) examinations in May 2003. These replace the established Professional Qualification Scheme (PQS) exams, which candidates have been sitting for some years. In many cases the content of the syllabus (i.e. the professional standards which the examinations test) has been updated or substantially revised. This is not the case for the Core Management subjects such as Managing in a Business Context. Our standards were reviewed and updated a few years ago, so past PQS papers dating from 1999 to 2003 will still be relevant for you to use as revision aids. As far as Managing in a Business Context is concerned, the change from PQS to PDS has principally meant a change in the style and structure of the examination paper.

This section starts by setting out the ways in which PDS papers differ from their PQS predecessors. The second part then explains the aims and thinking behind the setting of Managing in a Business Context papers in particular. This should help you to plan your revision more effectively. It will give you a good idea of what to expect and an understanding of what examiners are looking for when marking the scripts.

■ PDS – how does it differ from PQS?

There are four key changes that make the new PDS papers distinct from the old PQS papers in terms of their structure, style and nature. These are as follows:

1 Number of Section B questions

The most significant structural change concerns Section B. The PQS paper required candidates to write short answers to 8 compulsory questions over the course of an hour. On PDS papers the number of questions you have to answer has been reduced from eight to seven, and these are to be chosen from a list of ten.

This means that there will be fewer situations in which people are forced to embark on a question that they do not really know the answer to and have to try and improvise an answer. It also means that there will also be a few minutes more available for each question. However, as a result the expectations of examiners will be higher too. We will be expecting more assured answers to be provided by candidates and will be less indulgent to those who do seem to be improvising.

Section A stays the same as before in terms of its general format. For Managing in a Business Context this means that PDS candidates will be required to answer two longer essay-format questions from a choice of four. Section A, like Section B, is expected to take around an hour to complete.

2 Situational questions

The other very obvious change is in the style of the questions we are going to ask in both Sections A & B. In the vast majority of cases on PDS papers these will be situational. That is to say they ask you to assume that you have been placed in a particular situation and will ask you to respond accordingly. So, whereas on a PQS paper you would have got a straight question testing your knowledge of a subject area, the question will now be framed differently – you are giving a talk, you are asked to brief your CEO, you get into a debate, you receive an e-mail – requiring you to think not just about your subject knowledge but also about the context in which that knowledge may have to be deployed.

3 The thinking performer

The new-style PDS papers are intended to support CIPD's desire to admit to membership people who can demonstrate the ability both to THINK and to PERFORM as personnel professionals. The ability to do both these things has always been something that candidates have had to make evident in their examinations, but PDS papers reflect this concept of the 'thinking performer' more explicitly than has been the case before.

So when answering the questions you need to be able to convince the examiner that you both know what to do and can articulate good justifications for your actions / views. The key competencies of the thinking performer are as follows:

- personal drive and effectiveness

- people management and leadership

- business understanding

- professional and ethical competence

- added value

- continuing learning

- analytical and intuitive/creative thinking

- customer focus

- strategic capabilities

- good interpersonal skills.

Some of these are more readily tested via an exam than others, but it is useful for you to appreciate that these are the kinds of quality that the exams are intended to test for. Successful candidates will thus use the examinations as a platform to demonstrate that they have these characteristics.

4 Postgraduate standards

CIPD exams have always notionally been set at and marked at a postgraduate standard. However, in practice, it is fair to assert that this has not always been the case. At the upper end the answers we read are at this level, but it has been possible for people who have not demonstrated postgraduate capability to pass.

The PDS scheme is designed to be more clearly set at the postgraduate level and is being marked accordingly. In practice this means that the following are key to successfully passing your exams:

- You need to be able to demonstrate comprehensive understanding of the topics in the standards derived from wide and appropriate reading.

- Your answers must be analytical and not descriptive, critical and not celebratory.

- Your answers must be evaluative and not simply prescriptive. Don't just say what should be done in a particular situation but say why this course of action has been chosen

- We are looking for an awareness of how different elements of the standards integrate with one another.

- You should be able to demonstrate that you can undertake (and indeed have undertaken) independent learning. Candidates who simply swot up the contents of the course textbook, without undertaking any further reading, will thus struggle to pass.

There are two particular consequences as far as PDS exam papers are concerned:

- The questions will specifically ask for evidence to be provided to back up points – we want you to show us that you have been reading widely, that you are aware of current debates and have formed a view based on evidence from your learning.

There will thus be less emphasis than in PQS papers on you telling us what your own organisations are doing and greater focus on the literature and on reading you undertake about other organisations and alternative possibilities.

- In marking we will be looking for evidence of depth and breadth of understanding and will want good justifications to back up your arguments.

■ The Managing in a Business Context (MBC) exam

What is the thinking behind the choice of questions that form the MBC examination?

Apart from those that are set out above a number of different principles are adopted that are common across all the PDS papers. The following are the most important:

1   Each paper contains a mix of questions which, in combination, broadly cover the CIPD's established standards for the MBC subject area. The full list of standards is available on the CIPD's website. There are eight principal categories:

   –   the political system/governmental environment

   –   the legal system

   –   the economic environment

   –   technology

   –   international issues and developments

   –   social and demographic trends

   –   ethical matters

   –   the formation of business strategy/organisational interaction with the environment.

   All these areas will be covered at least once on the paper, some twice either in Section A or in Section B. Most questions relate specifically to one of these areas, but sometimes a question will be asked that draws on knowledge from two or more of these areas. For example, in May 2003, one question asked about the ethical dilemmas faced by firms expanding into developing countries (ethics and international issues) and another about factors affecting property prices, which potentially drew on material on the economic, political, demographic and social environments.

2   The focus of the questions will also be mixed. Sometimes we ask about your own organisation and its interaction with different elements of the external environment. Others are entirely focused on the business context itself and make no mention of your own organisation. In between are questions that focus on 'your industry' or on a specific economic sector such as the public sector or multinational enterprises. Some Section A questions will focus on more than one of these alternative arenas by asking a question in two or three separate parts.

Many candidates find the questions that focus on their own organisations the most straightforward. They thus tend to be those that are answered most frequently and at greatest length. However, as examiners we cannot set too many such questions. The CIPD qualification is intended to prepare you for a personnel career that may very well take you to organisations operating in wholly different industries or sectors than is the case with your current employer. It is only by asking questions about the business environment generally (i.e. as it affects all organisations) that we can test your preparedness to work effectively beyond your current industrial sector.

3   Some questions are tougher than others. In Section A there is usually one question that is judged by the examiners to be more straightforward and that draws on less specialised knowledge than the other three. The same principle is carried through into Section B, where one or two of the questions should pose no difficulties at all, while others will be a great deal more challenging because they test quite specific elements of the standards.

The purpose here is to provide a means of distinguishing effectively between the performance of different candidates. The more straightforward questions help us to determine whether a candidate should pass or fail. Someone who struggles with these is unlikely to pass the paper as a whole. However, in setting an exam that will be taken by a huge variety of candidates from a range of institutions we also need to be able to distinguish between candidates who are worthy of a 'pass' and those who should be awarded higher marks and perhaps achieve a 'merit' or a 'distinction' mark overall. The tougher questions are aimed at helping us as examiners to spot the strongest candidates and to reward them in a fair way. Someone who opts for the tougher questions and performs well when writing answers is thus maximising their chances of achieving high marks.

The same principle applies to multi-part questions. Often, where there are two or three parts to a question some will be more straightforward to answer than others. The weaker candidates will have no difficulty with the less demanding aspects, but will struggle to write full and well-informed answers to those parts that are more challenging. By contrast, the strongest candidates will write well-informed and comprehensive answers to all parts.

4   As far as is possible given the time lag between the time that the paper is set and the date that it is sat by candidates, questions that are topical will be included on the paper. This does not mean that questions focus on last week's news stories or indeed any specific news item, but attempts are made to include questions that are likely to be high on the news agenda in general terms at the time candidates sit their papers.

The reason for this is that it provides a means of testing which candidates are keeping themselves up to date with developments in the business environment while they are studying for their CIPD qualification. Continuous professional development (CPD) is a central feature of CIPD membership, and is something that all members of the Institute are expected to engage throughout their professional careers. It is thus important that student members get into this habit and accept the need to keep up to date with evolving issues and debates. Topical questions help us to distinguish between candidates who are keeping up to date and those who are not.

Irrespective of the precise question, however, the ability to articulate up-to-date points and to display a good understanding of contemporary thinking is something that examiners are looking for and will reward with high marks.

GUIDANCE TO CANDIDATES FROM CIPD EXAMINERS

This section draws on past examiners' reports to advise you on how to prepare effectively for the Managing in a Business Context paper. It sets out the common reasons that cause candidates to trip up and the characteristics that the best answers have in common. Finally, some 'golden rules' are set out for you to follow when planning and undertaking your studies in this area. Copies of past examiners' reports are available on the CIPD's website and will also have been retained by your college tutors, who always receive them in the post. Reading these, PQS as well as PDS, will help you prepare more effectively.

Common reasons for failure

1 Not answering the question asked

It is very common indeed for candidates to ignore the question on the paper and to write an answer to a question they think we should have asked instead. Sometimes the answers given are well-informed, lengthy and original, but nonetheless cannot be awarded many marks.

Sometimes this occurs by accident. Under the pressure of exam conditions a candidate misreads or misinterprets the question asked and heads off in a wrong direction. To avoid this happening it is vital to read the question clearly and to make quite sure that you answer it directly.

On other occasions it happens because a candidate does not know the answer to the question that has been set, so resolves to try to pick up some marks by writing an answer on a related theme that they do know something about. Another common type of answer is one that addresses a question that we asked on a past paper. This indicates that a candidate has prepared a great answer for a practice examination and is looking for an opportunity to re-use the material.

You are strongly advised to avoid falling into these traps. Not only are few marks awarded for answers to questions not set, but taking such a course of action firmly indicates to the examiner that you are not well prepared for the paper generally. It is thus taken as evidence of weakness. It is far better to write a short answer that does answer the question, or at least comprises a good stab at an answer, than to write many pages of material that are largely irrelevant.

2   Ignoring parts of a question

Another common reason that candidates drop marks is the tendency to answer a question only partially. We suspect that this often occurs because time is running out and the candidate is keen to move on to another question. However, it is often the toughest part of a question (e.g. the bit that asks you to justify your answer or to cite research evidence) that gets forgotten, so it may simply reflect the fact that the candidate is unable to provide a convincing answer to all parts.

Either way, it is important to avoid falling into this trap. As a general rule marks are allocated evenly across the different parts of a multi-part question, so failing even to attempt one part is a sure way of losing marks. You need to pace yourself properly so as to ensure that you give yourself sufficient time to address all parts to the best of your ability. An attempt at all parts, even if some aspects are weak, will be rewarded more than an answer which ignores one or more parts.

3   Factual errors

The third most common reason for failure among candidates sitting MBC papers is a straight-forward lack of subject knowledge. This leads people to guess or improvise answers in the hope that their answer may get close to the accurate one.

No amount of good examination technique can help here. There is no alternative but to ensure that you are properly prepared and that you have revised extensively.

4 Brief answers

While it is true that a short answer that addresses the question asked will gain more marks than a lengthy one which does not, it remains the case that people who are able to write full answers are a great deal more likely to pass than those who keep their answers very short.

Handwriting size varies considerably, so it is difficult to give comprehensive guidance on the length that answers should aim to be. The requirements of the questions themselves also vary a lot – particularly in Section B. However, as a general rule of thumb, you would be advised to aim to write at least four sides when answering Section A questions and at least three-quarters of a page when answering Section B questions. While it is possible to pass the paper by writing less than that, you need to be aware that most successful candidates write that much or a good deal more.

That is certainly the case with answers that are marked at the merit or distinction level. It is the only way to give a full and proper answer to the questions asked. It is not uncommon, for example, for candidates to write five or six sides in answering a Section A question and a side and a half for Section B questions.

5 Too great a focus on P&D issues

You need to remember that the MBC paper is about the business environment generally and not just those bits of it that have particular significance for P&D people. There is a tendency for some questions to focus on matters of particular interest to the P&D function (e.g. on the May 2003 paper there were questions on Employment Tribunals, labour markets, NVQs and equality issues), but others are quite deliberately intended to be answered from a general management perspective.

Some candidates forget that this is a Core Management paper and draw exclusively on P&D issues when answering questions with a far wider focus. Marks are lost as a result.

An example might be a question on business ethics that is answered entirely with a focus on the treatment of employees. The same is often true of questions about stakeholders, strategy making, technology and legal matters. Candidates know most about the P&D aspects of these topics and so choose to write about them alone. It is important to avoid this. It is quite reasonable (and indeed expected) that you will display a good knowledge of P&D implications, but you must take care not to focus on these exclusively or so heavily that non-P&D aspects do not get covered properly.

6 A failure to justify

A key attribute of answers that we judge to be of postgraduate standard is the presence of a good, solid, convincing justification to back up the points being made. Another common reason that people lose marks is a failure to do this or a failure to do it effectively.

Many questions on the MBC paper ask you in some shape or form to advance a view, to pass a comment on something or to argue a case. This is as true of Section B questions as it is of the longer Section A questions. Where this is the case it is essential that you not only state what you think but also say why – ideally by justifying your point of view with a good business case.

7 Making the same point more than once

This is a common fault, especially where a Section B question asks you to make 'five distinct points' or to cite 'three factors'. The candidate repeats the same basic point more than once using different terminology, but not really offering as second or third points anything very different from what was offered the first time round. The key here is to think as broadly as you can, drawing on knowledge you have gained from across the standards if necessary.

■ Common reasons for the awarding of high marks

1 Originality

As examiners it is always good to be surprised by an answer – to mark one that stands out from the crowd because it says something different. Provided such answers are factually accurate and are well justified they are rewarded well. Examples are answers that take a critical line. This shows that a student has clearly thought about what they have studied and has reached his / her own conclusions. Answers in which candidates are critical of aspects of their own organisations are particularly welcome because the tendency of most candidates is to boast about their own organisations' activities in an uncritical way.

2 Being up to date

Another way in which candidates pick up marks is by showing clearly in their answers that they have been reading newspapers and following news stories up until the date of the examination. Of course, this should only be done where it is appropriate – you will not be rewarded if you fail to address the question asked in a bid to include recent material – but where a recent news item or topical debate is clearly relevant to the question it can only help to include it.

3 Additional material

The better candidates are always able to go beyond the question asked and to offer further evidence of their knowledge when the opportunity presents itself. This means that they answer the question fully and accurately but then go on to add some remarks of their own, passing comment or offering further information *in addition*. Such candidates do particularly well because they have learned to see exam questions as an opportunity to show off or as a platform on which to display the full extent of their knowledge and understanding.

4 Examples and references

Stronger performers are able to justify their point of view by making reference either to published sources or to examples from their own experience. Such answers are rich in information and can be used to show the extent to which a candidate has read widely and thoughtfully.

5 Acknowledging different perspectives

Another characteristic of strong answers to MBC exam questions is the ability to survey a debate or issue by taking account of several points of view. This does not mean that it is necessary to give equal credence to all perspectives. You are still encouraged to come down on one side or another and to justify your case. But it is impressive when someone does this while taking full account of opposing points of view.

6 Effective presentation

While no portion of the marks is reserved to reward strong presentation, it is nonetheless the case that a well-presented answer is likely to score highly simply because it provides the best possible platform for the effective display of knowledge and understanding. Highly marked answers thus tend to be clearly legible and, above all, very well structured. The points are made logically, one after another, use being made of underlining and sub-headings to separate out the various paragraphs. Strong answers to Section A questions also tend to end with a concise conclusion, summing up the argument that has been made.

■ Golden rules to follow

1 Read widely throughout your period of study. Do not just rely on the course text, but ensure also that you regularly read broadsheet newspapers or weekly news publications and keep abreast of developments in the business environment.

2 Ensure that you gain a good working knowledge of the CIPD's standards for Managing in a Business Context. If there is some aspect that you do not understand do not brush it aside, but ask or read around until you do gain a sufficiently full understanding.

3 Read the exam questions thoroughly, focus on what the examiner is really asking you to write about, and then write the best answer you can to the question that has been asked.

4 Use the exam and the questions that are being asked as an opportunity to demonstrate how wide and deep your knowledge and understanding are.

5 Introduce original ideas, critical perspectives and up-to-date material wherever it is relevant to do so.

6 Always ensure that you provide robust and credible justification to back up the views that you express in your answers.

• PRACTICE EXAM QUESTIONS

In this section you will find two PDS Managing in a Business Context papers to use in preparing for your coming examination. The first is the paper we set for the May 2003 examination. The second is a specimen paper that was written before the introduction of the Professional Development Scheme in 2002 as a means of introducing students and their tutors to the style and nature of questions they could expect to find included in the examination.

You might find it useful as part of your preparation to use one or both of these papers as a mock examination by 'sitting' them under examination conditions. If so, you will need to give yourself two hours and ten minutes to answer the paper. Alternatively you might find it more helpful simply to note down the major points you would make if faced with these questions in your actual examination. Either way you will find detailed guidance on the kind of answers we were looking for in Chapter 7 as well as observations on the major reasons that answers were given low marks. So you may well prefer to avoid looking at these until you have first tested yourself using these papers.

■ Practice paper 1

Core Management - PDS

MANAGING IN A BUSINESS CONTEXT

May 2003

Time allowed – Two hours plus ten minutes' reading time

Answer TWO questions from Section A and SEVEN of the ten questions in Section B.

Equal marks are allocated to each section of the paper. Within Section B equal marks are allocated to each question.

Questions may be answered in any order.

If a question includes reference to 'your organisation', this may be interpreted as covering any organisation with which you are familiar.

You are likely to fail the examination if:

- you fail to answer seven questions in section B

- you achieve less than 40% in either section.

SECTION A

Answer ANY TWO questions in this section. All questions carry equal marks.

1   You are sent by your organisation to make a presentation on a university campus to potential graduate recruits. A member of the audience asks you to explain how economic decisions taken at national government level affect your organisation.

   What would you say? Your answer needs to refer both to the direct and indirect effects. You also need to provide examples to illustrate your major points.

2   Your organisation is asked by the local Chamber of Commerce to provide a speaker to address a meeting about gender equality issues. You are asked to brief the senior manager who is going to make the speech. The literature publicising the meeting contains the following statement:

   Despite some thirty years of sex discrimination legislation, women in the UK remain underpaid in comparison to men and hugely underrepresented at senior levels in corporate and public life. Why does this situation persist? What can be done about it?

   What would you recommend was included in the speech? What research evidence would you present to back up your arguments? What comments and questions would you anticipate might be asked by people attending the meeting?

3   You see a TV programme in which a number of business leaders appear arguing that the UK's political parties are increasingly converging in terms of their outlook and policy agendas. As far as business is concerned, they argue, it makes little difference nowadays which party wins elections.

   The next day several colleagues who watched the programme discuss this point. You join in the debate by distinguishing between the current programmes of **two** political parties. What would be your main argument? What examples would you cite to give weight to your opinion?

4   You are asked to carry out a stakeholder analysis for your organisation for presentation to a group of managers in the form of a short report. Your brief requires you to explain how each individual or group you identify influences or constrains the process by which organisational strategy is made and operationalised. What would you write? What examples could you draw on to illustrate the validity of your main points?

SECTION B

Answer any SEVEN of the questions in this section. To communicate your answer more clearly, you may use whatever methods you wish – e.g. diagrams, flow charts, bullet points – so long as you provide explanations of these.

1   You get into a debate at work about property prices and the factors which make them rise and fall. Identify at least **five** separate factors which you consider to be significant. What evidence could you refer to in order to strengthen your arguments?

2   A senior manager returns from a conference at which reference was made to a 'PESTLE analysis'. She is unsure about what the term means or whether such an analysis would be useful to carry out for your organisation. Comment on the concept for her. How would a PESTLE analysis illuminate decision-making in your organisation?

3   A line manager in your organisation is unsure about the role and function of Employment Tribunals. He asks you to explain these to him. What would you say? How do they differ from the other courts that form part of the UK legal system?

4   A visiting manager from Africa is discussing the UK political system with you. He asks what is meant by the term 'the separation of powers' and what is its practical significance for the political system. What would be the major points that you would make?

5   A colleague is listening to her car radio when driving to work. She hears a reference being made to 'five economic tests' that the government is using to determine whether or not the UK joins the Euro. On arriving at your workplace she asks if anyone knows what they are and what they mean in practice. How would you respond?

6   You are asked to explain how practice in the field of pension provision is affected by an ageing population. What would you say and why?

7   You are invited to write a short article for your local CIPD branch newsletter setting out the ways in which employment markets are likely to be affected by technological developments. What **three** distinct points would you seek to make? What evidence could you cite to back up your views?

8   You are present when a debate breaks out between colleagues about the major ethical dilemmas faced by organisations when they expand their operations into developing countries. You are asked to contribute your views. What would you say and why?

9   The HR director in your organisation has heard that a rival organisation is making the attainment of NVQ level 3 and 4 qualifications a requirement for some promotions. You are asked to write a short briefing paper setting out what these qualifications are and why they have been promoted by the government. What would you say?

10 You read an article in a newspaper which argues that the growth in the number of single-parent families in the UK is a public policy issue and should not be a matter of concern for employers. The consequences are for government to deal with and not employing organisations. You decide to write a letter to the newspaper's editor setting out your views on this question. What would you say and why?

■ Practice paper 2

Core Management - PDS

MANAGING IN A BUSINESS CONTEXT

Specimen Paper - 2002

Time allowed – Two hours plus ten minutes' reading time

Answer TWO questions from Section A and SEVEN of the ten questions in Section B.

Equal marks are allocated to each section of the paper. Within Section B equal marks are allocated to each question.

Questions may be answered in any order.

If a question includes reference to 'your organisation', this may be interpreted as covering any organisation with which you are familiar.

You are likely to fail the examination if:

- **you fail to answer seven questions in section B**

- **you achieve less than 40% in either section.**

SECTION A

Answer TWO questions from this section. All questions carry equal marks.

1   You are asked by your manager to write a section of an induction handbook to be given to new staff in order to help familiarise them with the organisation. She asks you to identify **three** separate technological developments which are currently affecting the business context in which your organisation operates.

You are further requested to explain what changes they have caused to date and to outline their likely future impact.

Thirdly, you are asked to state in what different ways these technological developments are affecting particular groups of organisational stakeholders.

What would you write?

2   Assume that you have been asked to give a talk lasting for around an hour to a meeting of your local CIPD branch. The topic is as follows:

'Demographic trends in the UK – a cause for concern?'

Write an outline of your talk together with a statement of your conclusions that could be distributed as a handout for participants. Justify your choice of content.

3   Assume that you are required to attend a meeting of senior managers in your organisation as the representative of the P&D function. During the meeting someone argues that the sheer volume of employment legislation is now so great as to have a severe impact on the ability of British organisations to compete internationally. Others disagree.

You are asked to set out your considered views on this issue and to justify them.

4   You read an article which argues that there is no sustainable business case for ethical organisational practice. 'At the end of the day', it says, 'businesses which act unethically are more successful than those who sing and dance about their ethical stances.'

You decide to write a letter to the journal in which the article was published setting out an alternative point of view. What would you want to say?

SECTION B

Answer SEVEN of the ten questions in this section. To communicate your answer more clearly, you may use whatever methods you wish – e.g. diagrams, flow charts, bullet points – so long as you provide explanations of these.

1 A senior manager is giving a talk at a local college on the different activities that organisations carry out in order to implement their business strategies. What would you expect him to include in his talk?

2 A colleague is reading a newspaper. He asks you to explain what is meant by the term 'monetary policy' and what it is all about. He also wants to know what are the major tools used by governments in operating monetary policy. What would you say?

3 Your manager reads about a new European Union Directive which may well have a considerable impact on P&D practices in your organisation. She asks you to describe what a Directive is and through what processes it becomes law. How would you respond?

4 You work for a small, but fast-growing organisation. The Chairman hears a speaker at a conference talking about 'corporate mission statements'. He thinks the organisation should have one but doesn't know what their purpose is or what elements typically make them up. What advice would you give him?

5 A visiting manager from China wants to discuss with you the merits of liberal democratic political systems. What points would you be keen to get over and why?

6 You work for an organisation that is about to start expanding overseas for the first time. You are asked to brief managers about the similarities and differences between the world's three largest regional economic groupings. What would you say?

7 You are present when an argument breaks out between colleagues about the relative merits of the state and private education systems. You are asked to comment on the purposes served by the state system. What points would you make?

8 You are asked to give a talk on the ways social attitudes towards work and the workplace have changed in the UK during the last twenty years. The organisers also want you to explore why these changes have occurred. Draw up a short plan indicating what you would say.

9   Your manager reads an article in a trade journal which states that a competitor of your company has been reported to the Competition Commission (formerly the Monopolies and Mergers Commission). You are asked to explain what this body is and what its functions are.

10 You get into a debate at work about the development of political life in the UK. Someone argues that political influence in the future will lie more with political pressure groups than with political parties. You are asked to comment on the methods used by such pressure groups to influence the direction of public policy. What would you say and why?

FEEDBACK ON EXAMINATION QUESTIONS

In this chapter brief feedback is given about each of the questions included on the May 2003 paper and on the specimen paper presented in Chapter 3. Inevitably, given that the May 2003 paper was actually sat by several hundred students and subsequently marked, rather more detailed feedback can be provided about where candidates scored well and where they tended to go wrong than is the case for the specimen paper.

If you have written answers or answer plans to these questions you will find it useful to compare what you have written with the feedback provided here. This will help you identify any obvious gaps between what the examiners were looking for and what you wrote. You may find it useful to revisit the questions a week or two after reading the feedback and having done some more reading to see how far you can improve your performance.

No model answers are provided here. This is so that nothing is done to give the impression to candidates that there are definite right and wrong answers to the questions on Managing in a Business Context papers. If we ask you to cite **five** factors in explaining some issue or to provide **three** reasons for a contextual development this does not mean that we have specific points in mind that we require you to make. All that is required is that you answer the question by making the required number of points. Provided that they are valid and distinct from one another it is for you to choose exactly which points you make. The fuller, more original and well-informed your answer the higher your mark will be. The same principles apply when we mark all the questions on the paper. We are looking for original, clear, well-written, thoughtful and (above all) knowledgeable answers to the question set. Except where the question is entirely factual in nature (e.g. B5 on the May 2003 paper), there are no 'expected' answers.

Instead more general guidance is given. In the case of the specimen paper this consists of ideas about the kind of answers we would like to see. In the case of the May 2003 paper the guidance draws on answers that we did see and marked highly as well as those that were less impressive.

■ MAY 2003 PAPER

Section A – Question 1

You are sent by your organisation to make a presentation on a university campus to potential graduate recruits. A member of the audience asks you to explain how economic decisions taken at national government level affect your organisation.

What would you say? Your answer needs to refer both to the direct and indirect effects. You also need to provide examples to illustrate your major points.

This question is principally intended to test your knowledge and understanding of aspects of your own organisation's economic environment. However, it also tests your ability to explain the impact of decision-making in the field of government economic policy.

Clearly the answer you will write will depend very heavily on the type of organisation for which you work. The impact of decisions made by the Chancellor of the Exchequer or the Bank of England affect local government, for example, rather differently from a clothing manufacturer or a retailer. Moreover, different fields of decision-making will be more or less significant. The decision about whether or not to recommend entry into the Euro is not a major issue for most public sector organisations. By contrast the government spending round, which allocates funds, is a matter of central significance. In the private sector the significance of government decisions varies depending on the extent and nature of importing and exporting activity. Actions that affect exchange rates matter for an exporter much more (and more directly) than they do for an organisation whose business is mainly carried out within the UK. However, there are obvious exceptions, such as organisations that rely on tourist trade.

The question specifically asks you to focus on direct and indirect effects. This is the part of the question that allows the examiners to make a clear distinction between solid 'pass' answers and those that are deserving of high marks. The better candidates had no difficulty giving examples of ways in which government decision-making operated both directly *and* indirectly. They were also able to give clear, succinct explanations to demonstrate their understanding. Weaker candidates tended to focus on one or two major areas of significance for their organisations, but struggled to articulate the lesser 'indirect' types of impact.

Examples of the type of decisions that candidates focused on were as follows:

- the level of interest rates

- government spending levels

- taxation/national insurance

- government borrowing

- exchange rate policy

- the decision on Euro entry

- supply-side measures aimed at increasing employability

- state benefits/tax credits

- public sector pay settlements.

Any or all of these could form the basis of a good answer, and this is by no means comprehensive. What matters is that candidates attempting the question are able to convince the examiner that they understand exactly how decisions taken at government level impact on their particular organisations. The fuller and better-informed the answer, the higher the mark awarded.

The weaker answers to questions such as this tend to be overly narrow in their scope, perhaps focusing only on one area of government policy. Here, common examples came from employees of public sector organisations focusing wholly on grant allocation issues. While these are clearly crucial in terms of their direct impact, much more could be said in terms of indirect links between the organisational environment and national government economic policy. For example, if you work for the police or the prison service you cannot sustain the argument (as many try to) that government spending on your service is the only issue of significance here. Taxation policy, for example, will affect your staffing budgets, while the level of benefits and the effectiveness of measures aimed at reducing unemployment may well help determine how busy your service is going to be in future years.

Section A – Question 2

Your organisation is asked by the local Chamber of Commerce to provide a speaker to address a meeting about gender equality issues. You are asked to brief the senior manager who is going to make the speech. The literature publicising the meeting contains the following statement:

> *'Despite some thirty years of sex discrimination legislation, women in the UK remain underpaid in comparison to men and hugely underrepresented at senior levels in corporate and public life. Why does this situation persist? What can be done about it?'*

What would you recommend was included in the speech? What research evidence would you present to back up your arguments? What comments and questions would you anticipate might be asked by people attending the meeting?

This question focuses on gender equality issues in the workplace. In so doing it draws on two areas of the standards for Managing in a Business Context – significant social trends and the legal context. Candidates were expected to demonstrate some knowledge of both these, a task that a good majority managed without difficulty.

The key in a multi-part question such as this is to ensure that all parts of the question are answered in some shape or form. In this case there are two substantive issues to address:

- the fact that women are underpaid in comparison with men

- the fact that women are underrepresented at senior levels in the organisation.

The meat of the question requires you to state why this is the case, while making reference to the very limited success that legislation has had in achieving equality over three decades. The second part asks you to say what could be done to improve matters. Whatever you say must be appropriate for inclusion in a talk and there is also a requirement to anticipate questions.

This question, as is the case with many, is essentially in two parts, one of which is rather easier to answer than the other. Stating why women remain disadvantaged on average in the workplace is straightforward for anyone who has studied the subject. Putting a convincing case about what can be done to improve their position is harder. It requires more thought and is less readily answered with reference to books and articles that you will have read.

Again, examiners are not looking for any particular line to be taken. Provided you can make a credible case you are free in questions such as this to make whatever argument you wish to explain continued gender inequality at work as measured by these two benchmarks. Typical answers made reference to the following:

- occupational segregation between men and women

- continued discrimination against women

- career-limiting breaks taken from work

- inter-role conflict for women with family responsibilities

- a preference among women returners for part-time work

- traditional conceptions of male (breadwinner) and female (homemaker) roles

- a persistence of masculine management cultures.

In addition, the better candidates remarked on the difficulties associated with bringing equal pay and sex discrimination cases in practice, the onus being on the 'victim' to bring her case and to challenge her managers in court. Many also made appropriate reference to the relevant recent changes in the law, such as the introduction of equal pay questionnaires and the right to request flexible working.

On the question of future improvements only the best candidates were able to say something substantial. Many made quite vague points about a need to change attitudes and/or the need for organisations to adopt the diversity agenda. High marks were thus awarded to people who could articulate an original set of proposals that put meat on these bones. The need to reform the law to give it greater teeth was a theme of such answers.

The other way in which this question helps examiners to distinguish between the better and poorer candidates is in its requirement to state what evidence could be used to back up a case. Strong answers named sources, most made less specific reference to the Equal Opportunities Commission or to David Farnham's textbook or named no sources at all.

Section A – Question 3

You see a TV programme in which a number of business leaders appear arguing that the UK's political parties are increasingly converging in terms of their outlook and policy agendas. As far as business is concerned, they argue, it makes little difference nowadays which party wins elections.

*The next day several colleagues who watched the programme discuss this point. You join in the debate by distinguishing between the current programmes of **two** political parties. What would be your main argument? What examples would you cite to give weight to your opinion?*

Questions on the political and legal systems are never popular among candidates sitting the Managing in a Business Context paper, and this was no exception. Only a small minority attempted to answer Question 3 in May 2003. Those who did make an attempt, however, tended to do well.

For anyone who is informed about political developments and political debate in the UK in recent years this is a straightforward question. While it was possible to pick any two parties as the basis for an answer, all focused on the Labour and Conservative parties.

Again, the question has several parts, all of which have to be addressed in some shape or form. First, there is a need to focus on the evolution of the outlook and policy agendas of the two parties chosen. Are they converging? How do they remain different? Secondly, there is a requirement to focus in particular on the effect that a switch in governing party has for businesses. Finally, the question asks you to cite evidence to back up your main argument.

Answering this question well first requires you to state what your principal position is going to be (i.e. your 'main argument'). Do you think that the Labour and Conservative parties are converging, are not converging or are converging only to a rather limited extent? Any position is acceptable to the examiners: what matters in terms of picking up marks is that you provide a coherent, well-informed and well-justified argument to back up your position.

The most commonly held view is that a high degree of convergence has occurred over the past ten years, the Labour Party abandoning most of its previous policy positions and moving on to political ground traditionally occupied by the Conservative Party. The rhetoric may be different, but the actual outcomes are not very different – or at least a great deal less different than they were a few years ago. Candidates arguing this case pointed to some of the following examples to back up their points:

- active acceptance of privatisation

- the adoption of monetary policy as the principal tool of economic management

- American-oriented foreign policy

- distancing from trade unions

- tough rhetoric on law and order issues

- tolerance of growing inequality between rich and poor

- strict control of public borrowing.

However, there remain major differences between the political parties on quite fundamental issues. Strong candidates could also identify these, display a good understanding of the key points of dispute and explain their significance. Examples are the following:

- devolution of power from Westminster to the Scottish Parliament and to regional assemblies

- the tone and nature of the relationship with the European Union

- orientation towards government spending and some aspects of public services reform

- attitude towards employment regulation

- position on issues such as the significance of marriage, gay rights, single parents etc.

Other candidates took the view that while there was extensive convergence in terms of the policy agenda, there remain significant differences in fundamental outlook. Some of these answers tended to be a little dated and lacking in detailed justification. For example, there was a tendency to identify the philosophical differences between the parties pertaining prior to the election of the Blair government, and particularly its re-election. This question requires candidates to address recent developments and not simply to state the traditional position. Those who could not back up their argument with relatively recent examples scored badly here as giving 'weight to your argument' is a clear requirement of the question.

Specific attention also has to be given in this question to the impact on business of different parties taking power. Again a variety of views could be expressed, all entirely acceptable to the examiners, provided they are justified and well-informed. The weaker candidates wrote very little about this, or else ignored it all together. The stronger candidates wrote about regulatory issues, corporate taxation, investment in skills development and the Euro debate. All provide a good basis for arguing either that it does or does not make much difference which party is in power.

Section A – Question 4

You are asked to carry out a stakeholder analysis for your organisation for presentation to a group of managers in the form of a short report. Your brief requires you to explain how each individual or group you identify influences or constrains the process by which organisational strategy is made and operationalised. What would you write? What examples could you draw on to illustrate the validity of your main points?

This was the most straightforward of the Section A questions on this paper and was chosen by a very large majority of candidates. This is always the case when questions are asked that focus on students' own organisations and thus require relatively little demonstration of knowledge gained through studying the subject. That said, while it was easy to get a pass mark on this question, it was harder to score highly.

The question first requires students to demonstrate that they know what a stakeholder analysis is and can briefly draw one up for their own organisation. The precise content varies from organisation to organisation but will typically include managers, shareholders, customers, employees and suppliers. Some organisations, especially in the public sector, would also include the community and government among their stakeholders.

Having identified the groups and explained why they are stakeholders, the question requires you to focus on how each influences or constrains strategy-making. This is where the better candidates seized the opportunity given by the question to show off their knowledge about the formation and operationalisation of strategy in their organisations, linking it to the various theoretical models described in the course text. Not only were they able to show how a particular stakeholder group had an influence in the aims or outcomes of the strategy, they could also reflect authoritatively on ways in which the type of strategy adopted was influenced by stakeholders and why.

However, this was not a requirement in order to pass. All that was needed here was a good case with some practical examples showing how in practice organisational strategy was influenced by customers, suppliers, employees and so on. Provided candidates wrote at reasonable length and with knowledge and conviction about these influences, they secured pass marks.

Section B – Question 1

*You get into a debate at work about property prices and the factors which make them rise and fall. Identify at least **five** separate factors which you consider to be significant. What evidence could you refer to in order to strengthen your arguments?*

This question draws primarily on knowledge gained about markets and prices in the section of the standards relating to the economic environment. However, the requirement to cite five distinct factors also provided good candidates with the opportunity to draw on their knowledge of other parts of the standards too – notably relevant social and demographic trends.

The better answers thus included discussion of the some of the following:

- shortage/over-supply of housing in different areas

- increasing adult population/ageing population

- increase in one-person households

- interest rates

- unemployment levels/state of a local economy

- transport links in different areas

- proximity of desirable amenities, good schools etc

- relative health of alternative types of investment (e.g. stocks and shares)

- planning regulations/government policy on green belts etc.

The broader and fuller the analysis given, the higher the number of marks awarded. Simply listing five factors in bullet-point style is insufficient here because of the requirement to provide some supporting evidence. In most cases students displayed a knowledge of trends in property prices in the process, stating for instance that rises in prices over recent years have coincided with a period of low interest rates. The question also provided an opportunity for candidates to display their knowledge of up-to-date trends (prices had begun to fall in the South of England after years of steady increases from the winter of 2002). As always, accurate topical references were well rewarded because they demonstrate that students have continued to follow developments in the business environment and have not simply read what they have to in order to get through the examination.

Section B – Question 2

A senior manager returns from a conference at which reference was made to a 'PESTLE analysis'. She is unsure about what the term means or whether such an analysis would be useful to carry out for your organisation. Comment on the concept for her. How would a PESTLE analysis illuminate decision-making in your organisation?

This was probably the most straightforward question on the paper and was thus answered by virtually every candidate. It simply requires you to define a 'PESTLE analysis' and to comment on its usefulness both in general terms and for your organisation specifically.

Any question that invites you to 'comment' on something is providing you with the opportunity to say something original or indeed critical about the topic concerned. The best marks for this question went to candidates who were sufficiently confident to do this. Most, however, simply stated that they thought PESTLE analyses to be very useful and said why. Few failed this question, but those who did either could not recall what all the items in a PESTLE analysis were or failed to address one part of the question. A fair number, for example, simply ignored the requirement to reflect on the usefulness of the tool in their own organisational context.

There are some slightly different versions of PESTLE described in some books. Not all the terms in the acronym are always listed in the same way. Allowance was made for this, but the vast majority of candidates had no problem at all in setting it out as follows:

P – political

E – economic

S – social

T – technological

L – legal

E – environmental

In terms of comments what could be said? Well, as always, much depends on the particular organisation. But the common critical view would be that as a tool of environmental analysis PESTLE gives equal prominence to aspects of the business context that are not necessarily of equal significance to all organisations at the same time. It could also be argued that it omits specific mention of potentially significant contextual factors such as demographic trends and issues relating to globalisation.

Section B – Question 3

A line manager in your organisation is unsure about the role and function of Employment Tribunals. He asks you to explain these to him. What would you say? How do they differ from the other courts that form part of the UK legal system?

This is a question that should not cause any problems for aspiring personnel professionals, but as is always the case when we ask questions about the political and legal worlds, many find them difficult to answer accurately. In this case it was the second part of the question that caused most difficulties and led to many people losing marks.

What is the role and function of an Employment Tribunal? It is a special type of court set up to deal with matters relating to possible breaches of employment statutes (i.e. Acts of Parliament and regulations issued under Acts that regulate the employment relationship). Employment Tribunals also deal with some contractual matters, but most breach of contract cases are still dealt with in the county and high courts. As such tribunals form part of the civil court system.

How do Employment Tribunals differ from other courts? There are many points that could be made here. The following are examples:

i) In most cases Employment Tribunals consist of a three-member panel comprising the Chairman (a lawyer) and two panel members to represent employer and employee interests.

ii) In most cases there is a requirement to get a complaint in to a tribunal within three months of the incident about which the applicant is complaining. If this is not done the matter will be declared out of time.

iii) Rules of evidence are more relaxed in Employment Tribunals than in other courts, hearsay evidence being permitted, for example.

iv) Tribunal proceedings are relatively informal in nature compared to those in other types of court.

v) Anyone can represent anyone else in an Employment Tribunal. While lawyers are increasingly hired to take cases, it is quite possible to be represented by a trade union official, a friend or simply to represent yourself.

Those were the kind of points we were hoping candidates would make in answering the second part of the question. Many were unable to do so. A great many focused on how tribunals differed from criminal courts. Some good points were made in this context, but such analyses failed to consider the rest of the civil court system, which also differs from the criminal courts in the same way as tribunals do. Others avoided answering Part 2 altogether by simply explaining (often using a diagram) where Employment Tribunals fit in to the court system and to which higher courts appeals are made.

Section B – Question 4

A visiting manager from Africa is discussing the UK political system with you. He asks what is meant by the term 'the separation of powers' and what is its practical significance for the political system. What would be the major points that you would make?

As with all questions on political systems, candidates proved disinclined to attempt an answer to this, even though it is a very straightforward, factual kind of question that can be answered very quickly in a few lines.

The 'separation of powers' is the term given to the way in which different branches of government are separated from each other so as to ensure that no single branch becomes overly powerful. The three major 'powers' in this context are:

i)   the executive or government, which proposes legislation and national government policy

ii) the legislature or parliament, which passes or rejects proposals and holds the executive to account

iii) the judiciary, which interprets legislation and ensures compliance.

In practical terms separating these different types of power helps ensure that no one branch of government becomes over-powerful because checks and balances are built in to the system. This helps deter corruption and the abuse of power. It also helps to ensure that all people remain equal under the law (i.e. that the same laws are applied in the same way to everyone).

Stronger candidates would have the opportunity here to earn higher marks by making further observations or passing comments on how effectively in practice the doctrine of the separation of powers works in the UK. It is common, for example, for commentators to state that the executive in the UK (and particularly the Prime Minister) have become overly powerful *vis-à-vis* other branches of government over recent years – especially when the occupant of the PM's job can command a big majority in Parliament. Another source of criticism is the role played by the Lord Chancellor who, it is argued, should not be (as he currently is) a member of the cabinet, speaker of the House of Lords *and* the most senior judge in the country. His role tends to dilute the notion of a real separation of powers.

Section B – Question 5

A colleague is listening to her car radio when driving to work. She hears a reference being made to 'five economic tests' that the government is using to determine whether or not the UK joins the Euro. On arriving at your workplace she asks if anyone knows what they are and what they mean in practice. How would you respond?

This is the type of question that people either know or don't know the answer to. As such it serves to discriminate very effectively between stronger and weaker candidates. The stronger ones know the answer and pick up plenty of marks, while the weaker ones only answer the question because they cannot find sufficient other questions to answer and tend to guess wrongly.

This question was included in the May 2003 paper because the government had announced its intention to make a statement on the question of Euro entry in May or June. It was thus highly topical at the time that candidates were sitting the examination and helped to reveal who was up to date with their knowledge and who, by contrast, was not reading newspapers and following key developments in the business environment.

The five economic tests were as follows:

1   Are business cycles and economic structures compatible so that we and others could live comfortably with Euro interest rates on a permanent basis?

2   If problems emerge, is there sufficient flexibility to deal with them?

3   Would joining EMU create better conditions for firms making long-term investment decisions to invest in Britain?

4   What impact would entry into EMU have on the competitive position of the UK's financial services industry?

5   In summary, will joining EMU promote higher growth, stability and a lasting increase in jobs?

In practice we did not expect candidates to list these five tests in the above form, word for word, or in the order the government sets them out. It was perfectly acceptable to write something like the following:

1   What will be the effect on job creation/unemployment?

2   What impact would joining have on foreign investment?

3   Is the UK economy converging sufficiently with those in the Euro?

4   What would be the effect on the City of London?

5   Is their sufficient flexibility built into the Euro to enable countries to withstand shocks?

The better candidates went on, after explaining each test briefly, to pass some kind of comment. In so doing they were seizing the opportunity to earn marks by displaying the extent of their knowledge. As is always the case when we ask questions about the European Union and related issues a wide variety of views are expressed. So some criticised the tests for being too imprecise and open to different interpretations; others remarked that the only real test that the government was really interested in was whether it could win a referendum on the question of the UK joining the Euro; while others thought there was a good case for adding additional tests focusing on the possible costs/risks of remaining outside the Euro-zone. Any comments of this kind show clearly that a candidate is bang up to date in their knowledge of the issue and is rewarded well.

Section B – Question 6

You are asked to explain how practice in the field of pension provision is affected by an ageing population. What would you say and why?

Demographic trends feature as a topic in the CIPD's MBC standards and so always feature somewhere on every paper. Most candidates are well-prepared for this and also appear to find the subject interesting. So there were some good, well-informed points made in answer to this question.

All we were really looking for here was evidence that candidates understood what was causing 'population ageing' in the UK, or indeed elsewhere in the world, and that they could articulate how exactly this had consequences for the provision of pensions. The question does not specify any particular type of pension (state, occupational or private). So here again was an opportunity for stronger candidates to pick up marks by reflecting on all three.

The key point we were looking for was an appreciation of the fact that population ageing means more older people *and* fewer younger people in a population and that this has implications for the dependency ratio – i.e. fewer people of working age paying taxes or making pension contributions that support retired people who are drawing their pensions. We also wanted a sense that candidates understood that this was a long-term trend, the major consequences of which will hit us in future decades.

A common reason for failure here was a tendency for candidates to see the word 'pension' and for this to trigger a discussion of other issues in the pension field, which are interesting and important, but which do not comprise an answer to this question. Underfunding owing to falling stock markets and increased taxation were the major examples.

Section B – Question 7

*You are invited to write a short article for your local CIPD branch newsletter setting out the ways in which employment markets are likely to be affected by technological developments. What **three** distinct points you would seek to make? What evidence could you cite to back up your views?*

Candidates' knowledge and understanding of technological developments is an area that is tested in some shape or form on every MBC paper. Because technological trends are so diffuse and varied in their impact, it is typical for questions in this field to focus on 'your own organisation'. However, in this paper a more general question was asked about the impact of technological developments on employment (or labour) markets. This posed few problems for candidates who understood what the term 'employment market' meant, although many either did not or ignored that requirement in this question.

We were referring here to the market (or markets) in which employers buy and workers sell their labour, and then asking what effects are contemporary technological developments having on the way that they operate? Many different points could have been made, backed up with examples. The following (or something similar to them) formed the focus of most answers:

- increased demand for certain skills (e.g. computer programming)

- changing supply of skills (e.g. younger people entering the job market being computer literate)

- de-skilling in some industries (e.g. mathematical ability no longer a requirement of jobs due to technology)

- technology-led redundancies increasing the supply of people looking for jobs in some places and industrial sectors (e.g. printing, banking in recent years)

- greater specialisation requiring training investment on the part of employers (e.g. new machinery in manufacturing)

- developments in the ways labour markets themselves operate (e.g. web-based recruitment).

The greater the detail candidates went into in explaining each of their three points, and the better the examples given by way of evidence, the higher the mark awarded.

A common reason for people losing marks on this question, as with all those in which you are asked to make a set number of points, was a tendency to repeat the same basic point (albeit using different terminology) two or even three times. This is not acceptable where a question is clearly asking you to make distinct points.

Section B – Question 8

You are present when a debate breaks out between colleagues about the major ethical dilemmas faced by organisations when they expand their operations into developing countries. You are asked to contribute your views. What would you say and why?

This was quite a demanding question, which brings together two sets of MBC standards – those covering globalisation issues and those focused on business ethics. The question does not require that any particular number of points are made, although the fact that it is phrased in the plural (dilemmas) suggests that more than one is being sought. In fact this question was answered well, most candidates being able to articulate and explain several types of ethical dilemma arising from a situation in which a multinational expands into a developing country.

The major types of examples we were looking for were as follows, although candidates with a particular knowledge or experience of this field provided others that were more specific to their industries:

i) wage levels/accusations of exploiting poorly paid staff in developing countries

ii) lack of employment regulation (e.g. health and safety law) in some developing countries putting people's welfare at risk

iii) environmental questions/exploitation of natural resources

iv) impact in terms of jobs lost/not created in the home country with knock-on consequences for wage levels

v) more general points about globalisation and its impact on local cultures/cultural traditions.

It is important to note that there is an 'and why?' at the end of this question. Another common reason for failing is a tendency for candidates to ignore this requirement and simply to list a few points. This question asks you to explain exactly why your points represent an ethical dilemma of some significance. There is no need to write a great deal here, but more is needed than a simple bald statement of the dilemma you have identified.

Section B – Question 9

The HR director in your organisation has heard that a rival organisation is making the attainment of NVQ level 3 and 4 qualifications a requirement for some promotions. You are asked to write a short briefing paper setting out what these qualifications are and why they have been promoted by the government. What would you say?

This should be another very straightforward question for aspiring personnel managers, and most who tackled it did so effectively. There are two parts. The first basically asks you to define level 3 and 4 NVQ qualifications, the second to state why they are being promoted by the government.

Nearly all candidates attempting this question correctly stated that NVQ stood for 'National Vocational Qualifications' and that these were standardised national qualifications covering many different industries and professions, indicating that a person had reached a certain level of proficiency in some skill set or another. Quite a good proportion, however, lost marks because they wrote about NVQs generally and not the higher-level 3 and 4 qualifications in particular. Strong answers were also generally provided to the second part, candidates writing about the need to provide people with marketable skills to help maximise their employability.

Section B – Question 10

You read an article in a newspaper which argues that the growth in the number of single-parent families in the UK is a public policy issue and should not be a matter of concern for employers. The consequences are for government to deal with and not employing organisations. You decide to write a letter to the newspaper's editor setting out your views on this question. What would you say and why?

This last question on the paper was one for which no particular answer or even type of answer was sought. Candidates were being given something of a blank canvas to set out their response to a stridently expressed point of view about the growth of single-parent families (a key social trend). People were free to agree or disagree either partially or wholly with the view being expressed and to develop an argument to back up their position.

In practice, the vast majority of people answering this question took the view that employers had a great deal to offer single parents and that they were in a position (as well as if not more than the government) to help tackle some of the consequences. Many focused on the provision of flexible working, of childcare facilities and other family-friendly policy initiatives aimed at providing opportunities for single parents to combine work with family responsibilities. Training initiatives were also commonly mentioned. The better candidates put a business case to back up their assertions.

The most common fault here, as with other similar questions, was a failure to address the 'and why?' supplementary question. In other words, they did not justify their arguments effectively. There is a tendency for candidates to believe that the answers they give are self-explanatory and do not need justification. This is not the case. If a question asks for an explanation as to why you think a point is significant, you must give some kind of justification, even if it just a sentence or two.

■ SPECIMEN PAPER

Section A – Question 1

*You are asked by your manager to write a section of an induction handbook to be given to new staff in order to help familiarise them with the organisation. She asks you to identify **three** separate technological developments which are currently affecting the business context in which your organisation operates.*

You are further requested to explain what changes they have caused to date and to outline their likely future impact.

Thirdly, you are asked to state in what different ways these technological developments are affecting particular groups of organisational stakeholders.

What would you write?

The aim of this question is to test your ability to evaluate and explain the significance of developments in the technological environment as they affect your own organisation. The question effectively has four parts, each of which candidates would be expected to tackle:

i)   the identification of three distinct technological developments

ii)   an evaluation of their effect on the organisation to date

iii) an estimation of their likely future impact

iv)   an analysis of their likely effects on different stakeholder groups.

The question thus requires the identification of stakeholder groups (shareholders, customers, staff, suppliers, community etc) as well as the technological developments themselves.

Answers to this question would vary considerably depending on the industry in which the organisation concerned operates, its size and type of operations. Any technological developments could be included in the answer from those affecting specific manufacturing processes to those that are having a more general impact on all organisations such as internet, intranet, e-mail, and other information and communication technologies. Students would be free to focus on whatever type of impact they wish. The focus could be on structural and cultural issues, on business policy, the competitive climate, impact on the outlook for investment, the regulatory environment, labour markets or management control.

While some treatment of HR issues would be anticipated, it is necessary on the MBC paper for students to show an ability to discuss issues that fall outside the specialist purview of P&D professionals. The broader and more informed the answer, the higher the marks that would be awarded. Where students speculate about the likely future impact of technological developments it is necessary to provide a brief (but convincing) justification to back up their arguments.

Section A – Question 2

Assume that you have been asked to give a talk lasting for around an hour to a meeting of your local CIPD branch. The topic is as follows:

'Demographic trends in the UK – a cause for concern?'

Write an outline of your talk together with a statement of your conclusions that could be distributed as a handout for participants. Justify your choice of content.

In marking answers the examiner would be looking for the following:

i)   an accurate description of the most significant current demographic trends in the UK

ii) an evaluation of their likely impact on organisations in the future

iii) an effective justification of the arguments deployed, particularly in respect of the conclusion

iv) an appropriate structure for the proposed talk.

The fact that the talk is to be given to a CIPD branch meeting indicates that human resource issues need to be included and could justifiably account for most of the content of the talk. Ideally the examiners would like to see evidence of a good knowledge of birth and death rates, the size and age profile of the working population, dependency ratios, geographical concentrations of population, as well as the gender and ethnic make-up of those either in or seeking work. Future issues could include a reduced supply of younger workers, an older workforce age profile, pension issues, skills shortages, regional variations in the cost of living, management of diversity issues, and changed customer profiles.

In terms of the structure of the talk, this should be logical, aimed at an appropriate level, interesting, illustrated with examples and relevant to its audience.

Section A – Question 3

Assume that you are required to attend a meeting of senior managers in your organisation as the representative of the P&D function. During the meeting someone argues that the sheer volume of employment legislation is now so great as to have a severe impact on the ability of British organisations to compete internationally. Others disagree.

You are asked to set out your considered views on this issue and to justify them.

This is an example of a question that raises an important and prominent policy debate, inviting candidates to develop their own argument in response. The examiners would be looking for the following when marking this question:

i)   evidence of an understanding of the debate the question relates to, its parameters and relevance

ii) an appreciation of the main arguments and evidence deployed on both sides of the debate about the volume of employment legislation and its possible effects on competitive advantage

iii) a clear focus on the international context of the question

iv) the ability to develop and justify an original argument with examples.

The nature of the argument advanced is not relevant to the mark that is awarded. Students are free to argue in favour of the proposition in the question, against it, or could develop a balanced position. Alternatively they are welcome to question the assumptions in the question by arguing, for example, that employment legislation does impact negatively on national competitive advantage but that it is nevertheless justified in ethical terms. What matters is that some line of argument is advanced and that it is justified convincingly. The more effective and well-informed the justification, the higher the marks that would be awarded. For example, the evolution of European-wide approaches to employment legislation would be relevant to this question. The ability to explain how and why would be anticipated in stronger answers.

Section A – Question 4

You read an article which argues that there is no sustainable business case for ethical organisational practice. 'At the end of the day', it says, 'businesses which act unethically are more successful than those who sing and dance about their ethical stances.'

You decide to write a letter to the journal in which the article was published setting out an alternative point of view. What would you want to say?

This final Section A question allows you free rein to develop an original line of argument. The particular position you take up is unimportant in determining the mark. What we are looking for is the ability to articulate and justify that position effectively. The more robust evidence that can be deployed in doing so (published and personal experience), the better. The examiner would be looking for the following when marking this question:

i)   an understanding of the key strands that make up the business case for ethical practice

ii) an explanation of the major strengths and weaknesses in these arguments

iii) evidence (published or from personal experience) to illustrate and back up points that are made

iv) a conclusion stating the candidate's considered view (with proper justification).

It is important with questions of this kind that the candidate does not take too theoretical an approach when answering the question. Practical examples of the ethical dilemmas facing businesses should be used as the basis of the arguments that are developed. Here too, although HR issues are likely to form a part of any answer, they should not form its exclusive focus. Relationships with other stakeholders (especially customers and suppliers) are equally significant and should be given proper consideration.

A common fault in answers that concern business ethics is the assumption that merely complying with the law is in itself ethical. While the examiners accept that non-compliance is unethical, it is considered necessary for organisations to go beyond the strict letter of the law in their activities if they are to be labelled 'ethical' or 'socially responsible'.

Section B – Question 1

A senior manager is giving a talk at a local college on the different activities that organisations carry out in order to implement their business strategies. What would you expect him to include in his talk?

This is a straightforward question focusing on the key stages necessary in translating a formulated business strategy into operational practice. While there would be some flexibility in marking to account for different views and interpretations, the following would be expected to be covered in some shape or form in good answers:

- setting objectives

- formulating specific plans

- providing necessary financial resources

- providing necessary plant and equipment

- providing necessary human resources

- monitoring implementation

- evaluating implementation.

Top marks would be awarded to candidates who distinguished between the different forms of strategy identified in the professional standards (rational, incremental, reactive etc) and were able to relate their answers to these.

Section B – Question 2

A colleague is reading a newspaper. He asks you to explain what is meant by the term 'monetary policy' and what it is all about. He also wants to know what are the major tools used by governments in operating monetary policy. What would you say?

This is an example of a common type of Section B question in which candidates are asked both to define a term and to comment on the practical purpose or aim of the concept concerned. Here the examiner is simply testing the candidate's understanding of one of the major tools of government economic management. Acceptable answers would show an understanding of the concept of 'the money supply' and its interaction with inflation. The significance of inflation control as a government objective would be explained, perhaps with some analysis of the consequences associated with a failure to do so. Candidates would then be expected to identify the central bank lending rate and interest rates as the main tools of monetary policy, explaining how these impact on spending, saving and borrowing decisions. The clearer and more authoritative the answer, the higher the marks. All that is required here is a basic explanation of key processes. There is no need to describe the institutional arrangements used to determine monetary policy either in the UK or other countries.

Section B – Question 3

Your manager reads about a new European Union Directive which may well have a considerable impact on P&D practices in your organisation. She asks you to describe what a Directive is and through what processes it becomes law. How would you respond?

The aim here is to test your understanding of the major ways that law is made in the European Union – an issue of increasing significance as far as employment legislation is concerned. It would be expected that candidates would focus on the process by which a draft Directive drawn up by the European Commission is considered by the Council of Ministers, negotiated over, amended and then sent on to the European Parliament for approval, before being introduced into national laws by the legislatures in each member state. Better answers might also include explanations of qualified majority voting (QMV), the role of the 'social partners' in formulating draft Directives or a description of the institutions involved. Answers that also referred accurately to European regulations, treaty articles and/or the role of the European Court of Justice would be well rewarded.

This is a good example of a question where a flow chart could be drawn illustrating the stages of the legislative process. Doing so would save time and thus allow candidates to display additional knowledge of the topic area.

Section B – Question 4

You work for a small, but fast-growing organisation. The Chairman hears a speaker at a conference talking about 'corporate mission statements'. He thinks the organisation should have one but doesn't know what their purpose is or what elements typically make them up. What advice would you give him?

Quite a few explanations of mission statements could be acceptable as answers here, drawing on material in the standards relating both to strategy formation and business ethics. It is likely, however, that most answers would focus on the corporate mission statement as a concise and effective means of communicating 'strategic intent'.

Much of the question can simply be answered with a list of points (such as values, focus, ambitions, methods, culture, HR-orientation). The better answers would give examples to illustrate what each of these terms means in practice in the context of a mission statement. Additional marks would be awarded to those who went on briefly to discuss more critical perspectives.

Section B – Question 5

A visiting manager from China wants to discuss with you the merits of liberal democratic political systems. What points you would be keen to get over and why?

This is a straightforward question that should pose few problems to candidates who have studied the topic. All that is required is a list of key concepts, together with some explanation of their meaning and merits. These would include some of the following, expressed in some shape or form:

- multi-party political system

- freedom of expression/the press/parliamentary debate

- representative democratic institutions

- regular elections

- active political pressure groups

- the rule of law

- universal suffrage

- protection of minority interests

- separation of powers.

Section B – Question 6

You work for an organisation that is about to start expanding overseas for the first time. You are asked to brief managers about the similarities and differences between the world's three largest regional economic groupings. What would you say?

The three largest regional economic groupings, the EU, NAFTA and ASEAN, are specifically mentioned in the professional standards. Students should thus be prepared to explain their role and be aware of differences between the way each operates. Here the examiners are essentially looking for a list of similarities and differences between the three institutions, together with sufficient explanation to indicate that the candidate understands and can articulate these points.

The main points that candidates would be expected to make would be as follows:

Similarities between NAFTA, the EU and ASEAN:

- free trade areas

- aim to enhance regional economic growth

- the provision of mutual assistance/co-operation

- the promotion of peace through international trade

- to allow bloc negotiations in world trade agreements.

Differences between NAFTA, the EU and ASEAN:

- a political dimension is far stronger in the EU and its aims are more politically ambitious than is the case with ASEAN and NAFTA

- EU evolving into a single currency bloc as well as a free trade area

- NAFTA dominated by one very powerful member (the USA) with a dominant currency

- ASEAN has a faster-growing population and is made up recently developed countries, some of which are not liberal democracies.

Section B – Question 7

You are present when argument breaks out between colleagues about the relative merits of the state and private education systems. You are asked to comment on the purposes served by the state system. What points would you make?

In asking for 'purposes' rather than a 'purpose', the examiner is looking for an indication that candidates can identify a range of aims for government spending on education beyond the transmission of academic knowledge. The kind of additional points being sought are as follows:

- socialisation into societal norms and values

- the development of personal and interpersonal skills

- preparation for roles in later life

- provision of vocational skills and knowledge to allow economic participation

- a vehicle for self-development and self-fulfilment

- a means of ensuring that basic primary and secondary education are provided for all

- a means of ensuring that employers have access to the skills they require.

Section B – Question 8

You are asked to give a talk on the ways social attitudes towards work and the workplace have changed in the UK during the last twenty years. The organisers also want you to explore why these changes have occurred. Draw up a short plan indicating what you would say.

Questions on changing social attitudes such as this inevitably require some reflection on differences of experience and perception between the generations. There is also a danger that very broad-brush answers will be given, when the real picture is one of complexity and substantial variation. The best answers recognise this and avoid simplistic responses that suggest that everyone in a particular group shares the same social attitudes.

In the case of attitudes towards work, the evidence indicates that people are becoming less loyal to their employers, more instrumental and short-termist in their outlook, less trusting of management and that they feel a great deal less secure. They are also more demanding in terms of what they expect from an employer and are more likely to seek alternative work if their demands are not perceived as being met. People are becoming more ambitious for themselves, being less happy than they were to settle for work that does not stretch or interest them. Finally, there has been a substantial decline in interest in trade union activity and a collective outlook towards workplace relationships.

The reasons stem from the experience of working in the UK over recent years. Among the factors that the better answers would be expected to mention are the following:

- decline in opportunities for lifetime/long-term employment

- workplaces engaging in continual change/restructuring

- redundancy programmes in the early 1980s and 1990s

- decline in the effectiveness of trade unions

- increased use of temporary contracts, sub-contracting and casual work

- increase in inequality of incomes between well and poorly paid employees.

Section B – Question 9

Your manager reads an article in a trade journal which states that a competitor of your company has been reported to the Competition Commission (formerly the Monopolies and Mergers Commission). You are asked to explain what this body is and what its functions are.

The MBC exam paper usually includes at least one question such as this, testing candidates' knowledge of the purpose of a national or international institution. These tend to be questions to which the answer is either known or not. A common error is to confuse one institution with another where a number operate together to achieve the same kind of aims.

A good answer to this question would identify the Competition Commission as a government-sponsored body charged with investigating the extent to which particular organisations exercise unreasonable monopoly power in their industries. Cases are referred to the CC both by the Secretary of State for Trade and Industry and by the Director General of Fair Trading. Specific mention should also be made of situations in which two corporations are seeking permission to merge and cannot do so until an investigation by the CC has been completed and a recommendation made to the Secretary of State.

The function of the CC is to prevent one organisation from becoming so dominant in a particular market as to threaten the existence of free and fair competition. Examples of recent CC/MMC investigations, for example in banking and television, would enhance an answer and ensure higher marks were awarded.

Section B – Question 10

You get into a debate at work about the development of political life in the UK. Someone argues that political influence in the future will lie more with political pressure groups than with political parties. You are asked to comment on the methods used by such pressure groups to influence the direction of public policy. What would you say and why?

This is another straightforward question, which simply aims to test the your knowledge and understanding of an important element in the business environment. Here the examiners would be looking for evidence that you are aware both of the direct and indirect methods used by pressure groups to change or to prevent changes being made in public policy.

The direct methods include lobbying policy-makers (i.e. ministers, MPs, civil servants and others who have influence with ministers) and responding to government consultation exercises. Indirect methods include influencing public opinion by securing media coverage, seeking to gain influence though the funding of political parties and sponsoring events at party conferences. As with all Section B questions, good examples used to illustrate the points being made would attract higher marks.

● THE STANDARDS

The purpose of this appendix is to take you step by step through the CIPD's Standards for the Managing in a Business Context course. These in effect define the syllabus that you will have studied and should provide the framework that you use to revise. All examination questions derive directly from one or more of these Standards. The purpose here is to explain what each means in practice and to suggest sources of further information that you can use to supplement your knowledge and understanding of the topics covered. Reference will be made to the CIPD's course text (*Managing in a Business Context* by David Farnham) and also to the books that are included on the CIPD's library holding lists for this module. All of these should be available in your college library.

■ Rationale, Learning Outcomes and Indicative Content

The standards are conveyed under three headings: Rationale, Learning Outcomes and Indicative Content.

The Rationale sets out in very general terms the purpose of the Standards:

Rationale

'Organisations and those responsible for managing them are increasingly subject to environmental turbulence and uncertainty. The external contexts within which businesses, public services and voluntary organisations operate are no longer stable and predictable but increasingly volatile and subject to rapid change.

As a result, managers have to identify, devise and implement appropriate strategies to ensure organisational survival, plan to achieve their goals and objectives, and respond to market and contextual uncertainties. Managers also have to take account of the normative values and ethical standards within which organisations and society operate.

The overall purpose of this module is to identify, examine and analyse the major contexts within which organisations operate, indicating how managements respond to contextual diversity, continuous change and ethical ambiguities. There is considerable emphasis within this module on knowledge and understanding, rather than on skills and competencies.'

Learning Outcomes

The Learning Outcomes, listed in two parts, sum up succinctly what a candidate should have learned having studied Managing in a Business Context. The examination is the major method used to determine whether these learning objectives have in fact been met:

To be able to:

a) Assess current economic and market changes and their impact on organisations.

b) Undertake SWOT and PESTLE analyses and advise on the opportunities and threats arising from this.

c) Provide examples of how organisations are affected by political institutions and processes and how organisations can influence the policy-making process.

d) Advise management on the possible effects of government policies, legislation and European directives on organisations and their activities.

e) Report on projected demographic and social changes and their relevance for organisations.

f) Identify current technological developments and consider their significance for organisational stakeholders.

g) Identify and comment on indicative international factors affecting organisations.

h) Evaluate the ethical issues facing organisations in dealing with stakeholders.

To understand and explain:

a) The nature of strategy and the main elements within the strategic process.

b) The differences between strategic search, choice and implementation.

c) The ways in which strategy is determined.

d) Types of strategy adopted by organisations and the importance of strategic review, monitoring and benchmarking.

e) How the external environment impacts on private, public and voluntary organisations.

f) The concept of PESTLE and SWOT and the dynamics of the political, economic, social, technological, legal and environmental contexts on organisations.

g) The main features of the market economy, its structure and processes and their implications for organisations.

h) Interactions between political and economic systems, including the European dimension.

i) The changing social structure and its implications for organisations and their stakeholders.

j) The nature, sources and administration of law, especially contract, consumer, competition and employment law.

k) New technologies, their applications and implications for organisation stakeholders.

l) Globalisation and competing theories of economic change.

m) The relevance of business ethics and social responsibility for organisations and managerial decision-taking.

Indicative Content

The third heading is 'indicative content' which sets out in some detail, topic by topic, the areas that students need to study and that they may be examined on. In the case of Managing in a Business Context the indicative content is divided into three areas, a percentage figure being assigned to each as a means of indicating its broad weight within the standards as a whole. This figure should help you to plan your revision more effectively by ensuring that you spend the right amount of time focusing on each of the three parts:

1) Strategic framework (15%)

a) The nature and role of strategy and planning within organisations. Rational, incremental and reactive approaches to managing. The concepts of strategy, analysis and strategic search, choice and implementation. SWOT and PESTLE analyses. Mission statements, corporate plans and business plans. The actors in strategy determination and implementation. Constraints upon managing strategically: uncertainty, risk and human judgement.

b) Converting strategy into practice. Links between corporate and functional strategies. Business plans and operational and programme budgets. Integration of strategy and policies. Cascading processes. Monitoring and evaluating strategy. The concept of the learning organisation.

c) Organisational stakeholders (including owners, workers, customers, suppliers and communities) and stakeholder theory. The implications of stakeholding for corporate decision-making and strategy.

2) The external contexts of organisations (75%)

a) The economy: changing structure of the national and international economies. Types of organisations: businesses, public services and voluntary bodies. Markets, prices and market regulation. Role and functions of the state in the economy and economic management. European Monetary Union.

b) The political system: national and European institutional political structures. Forms of governance and democratic process. Citizenship. Roles of elections, political parties and pressure groups (including business and employee groups) in public policy formation. The legislative process.

c) Social structure: main demographic and social trends. Social stratification. Changing social attitudes, values and beliefs. Education, training and their relation to economic performance.

d) Legal framework: the legal system. Sources of law. Contracts: formation, application and enforcement. Legal protections for employees and consumers. Competition law.

e) Technology: new technologies and their impacts on people, organisations and society.

f) International factors: international institutions such as the World Bank, IMF, GATT, WTO and OECD. Transnational companies. Regional economic groupings (eg: EU, NAFTA, ASEAN). Globalisation and patterns of international trade.

3) Social responsibility and business ethics (10%)

a) Obligations of organisations to owners, workers, customers, suppliers, communities and the eco-environment.

b) Social responsibility and legal accountability.

c) Ethics and professionalism. Ethics and corporate stakeholders.

■ What does this mean in practice?

You can use the Standards as a framework for studying and revising the module, ensuring that you have notes on each area that is identified and that you fully understand the meaning of the various terms and concepts included within them.

The Standards also provide you with a good indication of the areas that you may be examined on when you come to sit your Managing in a Business Context paper. In essence they comprise eight distinct subject areas, which are weighted broadly equally in terms of their size within the Standards:

1) The strategic framework

2) The economic context

3) The political context

4) The social and demographic context

5) The legal context

6) Technology

7) International factors

8) Social responsibility and ethics.

You can therefore be sure that there will be *at least* one Section B question set on each of the eight areas and that six of the eight subjects will be represented twice either in Section A or in Section B. On some papers all these topic areas appear twice, maybe three times, in some shape or form through questions that draw on themes from two or more of them.

A guide to the Standards in each of the above areas is provided below, explaining what each comprises and suggesting sources of information that you can use when studying and revising. Subject areas derived from the Standards are delineated, which you may find useful as a basis for organising your notes and compiling a revision plan. You will see that there is some overlap between the different subject areas. This is inevitable because a number of important topics, for example, are part of both the social and economic contexts, or relate both to economics and technology.

■ Recommended reading

Reference is made to the following books, which make up the CIPD's recommended reading for students sitting the Managing in a Business Context examination.

General texts

FARNHAM, D (1999): *Managing in a business context*. CIPD.

BROOKS, I & WEATHERSTON, J (2000): *The business environment: challenges and changes*. Second Edition. FT / Prentice Hall.

CARTWRIGHT, R (2001). *Mastering the business environment*. Palgrave.

MORRIS, H WILLEY, B and SACHDEV, S (2002): *Managing in a business context: an HR approach*. Second Edition.

PALMER, A & HARTLEY, B (2002): *The business environment*. Fourth Edition. McGraw Hill.

Texts on specific topic areas

ABERCROMBIE, N & WARDE, A (2000): *Contemporary British society*. Third Edition. Polity Press.

ARTIS, M.J. (1996): *The UK economy*. Fourteenth Edition. Oxford University Press.

CAMPBELL, D, STONEHOUSE, G & HOUSTON, B (2002): *Business strategy: an introduction*. Second Edition. Butterworth Heinemann.

DICKEN, P (2003): *Global shift: reshaping the global economic map in the 21st century*. Fourth Edition. Paul Chapman Publishing.

HARRISON, A, DALKIRAN, E & ELSEY, E (2000): *International business*. Oxford University Press.

JONES, B et al (2001): *Politics UK*. Fourth Edition. Longman.

KEENAN, D & RICHES, S (2002): *Business law*. Sixth Edition. Longman.

MACMILLAN, H & TAMPOE, M (2000): *Strategic management: process, content and implementation*. Oxford University Press.

McCORMICK, J (2002): *Understanding the European Union: a concise introduction*. Second Edition.

TREVINO, L K & NELSON, K A (1999): *Managing business ethics*. Second Edition. Wiley.

[a new edition is due for publication in late 2003]

■ The subject areas

The strategic framework

1) Environmental analysis

The section of the Standards on strategy is the most comprehensive and is weighted rather more heavily than the other subject areas. You can therefore be certain that at least two questions on some aspect of the strategic framework will feature on any Managing in a Business Context exam paper. Particular emphasis needs to be placed on the ways in which organisations can analyse their business environment as this is the central concern of this set of Standards. The following list of headings may help to provide a framework for your revision:

- PESTLE analysis

- analysis of competitive position

- SWOT analysis

- portfolio analysis

- financial analysis

- skills and competence analysis

- strengths and weaknesses of these approaches.

2) Types of strategy-making

There is considerable debate about the nature of strategy-making in organisations and in particular about how formal and planned approaches are used in practice. It is not necessary for you to develop in-depth knowledge about these debates, particularly the more theoretical aspects, but you do need to gain a broad understanding of the main contours. The key topics are as follows:

- definitions of 'strategy'

- rational approaches

- logical incrementalism

- emergent approaches.

3) Stages in strategy-making

Another related topic area focuses on the various different elements that can make up the strategy-making process. From time to time questions are asked in exams that focus specifically on a particular stage, often asking you to discuss the way your own organisation operates in this respect. You therefore need to be able to show that you understand the significance of each major stage:

- external analysis

- internal analysis

- evaluation of strategic responses

- strategic choice

- implementation

- evaluation

- review.

4) Operationalising strategy

The implementation stage is especially important and will be one you are most likely to be involved in early in your career. It is also the area in which P&D professionals make the most significant contribution. You should thus be in a position to write with some authority on the following, focusing in particular on the people issues:

- effective change management

- setting objectives / cascading

- information and communication

- structural issues

- cultural issues

- mission statements

- budgeting.

5)   Constraints on strategy

The strategy-making process is rarely smooth. Getting it right is as much about devising methods of overcoming the barriers that get in the way as much as it is about devising a strategy. Indeed, several constraints act to prevent effective determination of strategies in the first place. You need to think about the constraints faced in your own organisation and more generally. The following are suggested areas to focus on:

- quality of information

- conflicts of interest

- cultural barriers to change

- ineffective leadership

- ineffective communication

- inertia / risk aversity

- financial constraints.

6) Stakeholders

Reference is made in the Standards to stakeholder theory and to stakeholder analysis relating both to the strategic framework and to social responsibility. It is thus particularly important to be able to discuss the different types of stakeholder with an interest in different types of organisation. You also need to be able to write about your own organisation's stakeholders. The link between stakeholders and strategy-making is explicitly made in the Standards. You may find it useful to organise your thinking around the following:

- defining stakeholders

- diverse interests and expectations of stakeholders

- the influence of stakeholders on strategy formation

- the influence of stakeholders on the implementation of strategy

- stakeholder mapping.

Sources of information

Farnham (Chapter 1) provides a solid introduction to the theoretical perspectives and also reflects on some practicalities relating to strategy. A more comprehensive treatment is offered in books that are wholly concerned with strategic management processes. Two of the more accessible titles are included on the CIPD's library holding lists. These are *Business strategy* by Campbell et al (2002) and *Strategic management* by Macmillan and Tampoe (2000). Both cover comprehensively all the issues raised in the Standards. Other introductions to the business environment include some coverage of strategy too, particularly environmental analysis. You will find it useful to refer to Morris et al (Chapter 3), Cartwright (Chapters 2 & 12), Brooks & Weatherston (Chapter 1) and Palmer & Hartley (Chapter 13).

The economic context

1) Major contemporary economic trends and their consequences for organisations

You need to be familiar with the most important economic trends affecting organisations today, their principal causes and their consequences in practical terms for the management of organisations. The following are among the most important:

- decline of manufacturing and the rise of the service economy

- privatisation of public corporations and private involvement in the provision of public services

- increased international trade

- tightening labour markets

- economic growth

- Inemployment

- inflation

- output

- productivity

- government spending

- exchange rates

- interest rates

- the financial markets.

2) The structure and workings of market economies

You need to understand how the UK economy is currently structured and the reasons for its recent evolution. Familiarise yourself with the major industrial sectors and different types of corporate governance, noting the key differences between the categories. The major areas would include the following:

- private firms

- public limited companies

- public corporations

- public services

- public-private partnerships

- voluntary organisations

- the stock exchange

- the extent and nature of economic competition.

3) Interaction between the political and economic systems

The way in which businesses and other organisations are regulated by government and the methods used by businesses to influence the development of government policy are matters that regularly feature in Managing in a Business Context examinations. So you need to be confident in your understanding of the major types of regulation that exist or could exist in the future, and of the various political lobbying activities that organisations undertake. The following is a list of key topic areas:

- market regulation

- regulation of monopolies

- major forms of state regulation of businesses

- deregulation

- regulation of privatised utilities

- EU intervention in markets

- business lobbying groups

- other ways in which organisations influence government actions.

4) Ways in which markets for goods, services and labour operate

Microeconomics is the study of markets for goods and services, the way they work and the major influences on their operation. It is necessary to grasp the basic principles of supply and demand, barriers to free competition, methods used to enhance productivity and profitability, and the major sources of finance. You need to pay particular attention to the operation of labour markets and their significance for organisations. You also need to be aware of how demand, supply and prices are determined in command economies in which regulation plays a greater role than is the case in the UK. Key topic areas are as follows:

- determinants of demand for goods and services

- determinants of supply of goods and services

- pricing policy

- money markets

- capital markets

- wages and other costs

- economies of scale

- command economies

- international trade.

5) Government economic policy

Another subject area that frequently appears on Managing in a Business Context exams is government economic management. You therefore need to gain a broad understanding of the major objectives government has as far as the economy is concerned and of the constraints within which ministers and their advisers are obliged to operate. What are the main tools of economic management that are available and what are the main arguments in favour or against their use? What are the direct and indirect consequences for organisations? You should be familiar with the following:

- the aims of government economic management

- limits on the ability of government to manage an economy

- the Keynesian and monetarist traditions

- controlling inflation

- minimising unemployment

- maximising growth

- balance of payments

- government spending / debt

- taxation

- labour market interventions.

6) European Economic and Monetary Union

The European dimension and its future development are the most significant long-term issues facing the UK economy today. The decision about whether or when to join the euro is momentous and is a topic about which you must develop understanding and opinions. However, Economic and Monetary Union has other dimensions too, which must not be forgotten. For example, there is the development of a single market, the evolution of social policy and the thorny issue of European-level regulation to consider. You should ensure that you have gained a broad understanding of the following:

- European Union involvement in economic management

- the Common Agricultural Policy

- the social dimension

- the single market

- arguments for greater / less EU intervention in economic management

- the case for UK entry into the euro

- the case against UK entry into the euro

- government policy on the euro.

Sources of information

Up-to-date information on these issues is best found in newspapers and journals. Each year in November *The Economist* publishes a guide to the coming year, which includes readable summaries and explanations of trends of this kind. Longer-term, underlying developments are covered by Farnham (Chapter 2), Cartwright (Chapters 5 & 12), Brooks & Weatherston (Chapters 3 & 9), Morris et al (Chapters 2, 4 & 5), Palmer & Hartley (Chapter 7) and much more thoroughly in the various chapters in the book edited by Artis.

The political context

1) UK political structures and institutions

Questions that ask you to explain the role and function of particular political institutions are commonly set as Section B questions. Candidates often have difficulty with these or try to avoid them. They are, however, quite straightforward and are a good source of high marks for those who do them well. It is thus worth spending some time coming to grips with the various institutions that make up the UK political system and the ways in which they interact with each other. The following is a useful checklist:

- local government

- devolved parliament and assemblies

- the House of Commons

- the House of Lords

- the Cabinet

- the Civil Service

- political parties

- the process by which statutes are made

- the electoral system.

2) EU political structures and institutions

Increasingly our law, especially that which relates to competition and employment, originates at the European level. This is reflected in the Managing in a Business Context exams, which invariably contain one or more questions that relate to European institutions or to the influence of the EU. You should therefore try to ensure that you can explain the role and function of the following:

- the major European treaties

- the European Commission

- the Council of Ministers

- the European Parliament

- the European Court of Justice

- the Economic and Social Committee

- European Directives.

3) Governance and citizenship

It is also common for questions to be asked that relate to the more philosophical aspects of politics. The Standards require you to be broadly familiar with different types of political system, and to be aware specifically of the major features of liberal democracies. The following is a list of topic areas:

- Liberal democracy

- Communist and post-Communist systems

- authoritarian systems

- citizenship

- rights and duties

- freedom of the media

- equality before the law.

4) Government policy

From time to time questions are asked about current government policies that may have an impact on organisations and particularly on employment matters. These tend to focus on topical issues, so it is difficult to give a straightforward list of the areas that may be covered. What is important is that you are able to state what are the major planks of the government's programme at any given time and that you can advance some views on these, either supportive or critical. The following are guidelines on the areas of government policy that have the most potential impact on organisations:

- policy towards the European Union

- economic policy

- employment regulation

- industrial policy

- education policy

- pensions and welfare

- pegional policy

- transport policy

- immigration and asylum

- housing

- the environment.

In addition, you should ensure that you are familiar with any area of government policy that affects your industry in particular. This will enable you to answer questions about the impact of policy on your own organisation with confidence and authority.

5) Influencing government

The final major subject area that is covered in the Standards on the political context concerns the lobbying of government and other means by which organisations and pressure groups seek to influence a political programme. The following are the main topics that you should revise:

- the role of political parties

- pressure groups

- trade unions

- employers' organisations

- the lobbying process

- the role of the media.

Sources of information

An excellent source of information on most aspects of British political developments, including those you need to know about for the Managing in a Business Context exam is *Politics UK*, edited by Jones, Kavanagh, Moran and Norton. New editions are issued every three or four years, so the coverage is reasonably up to date. The Fourth Edition came out in 2001, after the last general election. European Union matters – institutions and the major debates – are covered in greater depth by McComick (2002). Briefer treatments that focus specifically on the context for business can be found in Farnham (Chapter 3), Morris et al (Chapter 8), Cartwright (Chapter 4), Brooks & Weatherston (Chapters 7 & 8) and Palmer & Hartley (Chapter 8). As with the economic context, though, it is necessary to supplement what you read in these books with knowledge of unfolding events and debates. There is no substitute here for reading broadsheet newspapers and weekly news magazines, and watching TV news programmes.

The social and demographic context

1) Major current social trends

Questions on social trends are much more popular among candidates sitting the Managing in a Business Context exam than those dealing with economics, politics and law. They are invariably answered early on and more is written about them than other topics. The key trends to be familiar with are the following:

- the position of women

- the position of ethnic minorities

- marriage and family

- geographical mobility

- career patterns

- trade union membership

- political participation

- consumerism.

2) Current demographic trends

Developments in the demographics of the UK have important longer-term implications for employing organisations. It is thus important that aspiring P&D professionals are very familiar with the broad trends, their causes and their consequences. As with social trends, the questions that are set on demographic issues are generally well answered by candidates. Key points to focus on are the following:

- birth rates

- death rates

- immigration/expatriation

- age patterns

- geographical spread of the population

- the size and make-up of the working population

- implications for the welfare and pensions systems

- implications for the labour market

- implications for the education system

- general global demographic trends.

3) The social structure

Social trends concern the way we choose to live our lives, but these occur within a broader social structure that is evolving and being reshaped rather more gradually. These have profound implications for organisations, but are also determined to a great extent by employment and earnings patterns. The following list of points comprises the relevant subject areas that commonly feature on exam papers:

- social class

- social mobility

- occupational classifications

- income distribution

- the role of employing organisations in shaping social structures

- implications for organisations of changes in social structures.

4) Social attitudes

Social attitudes are continually changing and developing in new directions. They also vary considerably between different communities and generations. This is thus an area in which up-to-date knowledge is important. Nonetheless, it is possible to identify some of the more significant trends as a starting point for revision purposes:

- attitudes towards government, state institutions and the EU

- attitudes towards welfare recipients

- family and gender roles

- religion and morality

- crime and drugs

- work and employment

- health and fitness

- money, saving and spending

- discrimination vis a vis minority groups.

5) Education and training

The final major topic that appears in the Standards under the broad heading of the social context is education and training. Developments in this area are clearly central to the responsibilities of P&D professionals and thus regularly form the basis of exam questions. You need to develop an understanding of the following areas so that you can express an informed opinion if required:

- the purposes and consequences of education and training

- the school system

- the further and higher education systems

- government training initiatives

- inequality in education

- links between education and national economic growth

- political debates about education.

Sources of information:

All the above topic areas and a good many others besides are comprehensively summarised in the textbook edited by Abercrombie and Warde called *Contemporary British Society*. The Third Edition is the most recent, published in 2000. It is included on the CIPD's library holding lists, so you will be able to find a copy in your college library. In addition, all the texts on the business context in general contain one or more chapters on social and demographic matters. You will find it useful to read Farnham (Chapter 4), Cartwright (Chapters 3 & 9), Palmer & Hartley (Chapter 11), Morris et al (Chapter 6) and Brooks & Weatherston (Chapter 5). For current information about up-to-date issues of public interest you will need to read newspapers and journals.

The legal context

1) Sources of law

Questions with a legal flavour are often poorly done by candidates sitting the Managing in a Business Context examination. People steer clear of them when they can and tend to produce rather ill-informed answers when they are unable to avoid answering them. Gaining a good working knowledge of the workings of the law and how it affects organisations is thus a good way of picking up marks. You should start by becoming familiar with the different sources of law and how they differ from each other:

- statutes

- regulations issued under statutes

- European treaty articles, Directives and regulations

- common-law principles

- contract

- tort

- trust

- legal precedent

2) Legal institutions

The civil law is enforced by a variety of legal institutions. You need to know what types of cases go to which courts, how the appeals system works and have some knowledge of other agencies that play a role in the legal system. You also need to understand how the criminal law works, especially as regards the activities of employing organisations. The following are the key areas to focus on:

- the county and High courts

- the magistrates courts

- the Crown courts

- the Court of Appeal

- the House of Lords

- the European Court of Justice

- Small claims courts

- Employment Appeal (and other) Tribunals

- the Health and Safety Executive

- the Information Commissioner

- the Central Arbitration Committee.

3) The law of contract

Contracts are central to the employment relationship and to all commercial transactions. They are binding in law and can be enforced in a court if necessary. You need to develop an understanding of the principles of the law of contract in the UK and the way that contracts can be enforced. You will find it useful to focus on the following:

- the elements of a valid contract

- void contracts

- remedies for breach of contract

- the contract of employment

- express and implied terms.

4) Competition law

There is a fair amount of regulation concerning competition between commercial organisations emanating both from UK statutes and EU Directives. You need to be broadly familiar and able to comment in an informed way on the following:

- the purpose of UK and EU competition law

- restrictive practices

- monopoly power

- the major competition Acts

- the Office of Fair Trading

- the Competition Commission

- other regulatory bodies.

5) Consumer law

Another area of law that regulates the activities of businesses and any organisation providing goods or services is that which gives protection to consumers. This comes in a variety of forms and continues to develop. You do not need to develop any great expertise in this field, but it is necessary to understand how this body of law works in general terms:

- the Fair Trading Act

- the Trade Descriptions and Misrepresentation Acts

- regulation of the supply and sale of goods and services

- the Consumer Credit Act

- the Consumer Protection Act

- the Director General of Fair Trading.

6) Employment law

If you have not already done so, you will be covering employment law in some detail during your CIPD studies. As far as the Managing in a Business Context exam is concerned, the need is only to have gained a grasp of the key principles and the basic functioning of the major employment statutes. These include the following:

- unfair dismissal law

- discrimination law

- health and safety law

- family-friendly statutes

- data protection

- the national minimum wage

- deductions from pay.

Sources of information

Business Law by Denis Keenan and Sarah Riches is an excellent source of information about all the topic areas listed above. They bring a new edition out every three or four years. The Sixth Edition was published in 2002 and is thus reasonably up to date. Because the law develops and changes continually you may find earlier editions to be out of date in key respects. The legal institutions of the EU are assessed in McCormick (Chapters 4 & 5). Coverage in the general texts on the business environment is also extensive, each of the following containing a strong chapter on legal matters: Farnham (Chapter 5), Brooks & Weatherston (Chapter 7), Morris et al (Chapters 9–11), Palmer & Hartley (Chapters 6 & 9) and Cartwright (Chapter 10).

Technology

1) Major current technological trends

You are not expected to grasp the detail of current technological developments. They are far too many and varied to allow any reasonable examination question of such a kind to be set. However, it is important that you are able to display a broad understanding of the major contemporary trends, their purpose and origin, and most importantly their consequences for your industry and for employing organisations in general. The major trends to consider are as follows:

- developments in the field of information technology

- laser technologies

- biotechnology

- transportation

- telecommunications

- perspectives on the drivers of technological change

- different types of technological development

2) The impact of technology on organisations

Because technology is so diverse in its impact on organisations it is difficult to ask precise examination questions in this area. Instead, candidates are asked to explain how technologies are impacting specifically on their own organisations or on their industry in more general terms. Inevitably there is a tendency to focus on HR matters, but higher marks tend to be given to people who display an understanding of the broader impact of technological developments. The following are common examples:

- new product development

- manufacturing processes

- design and product development

- data storage and manipulation

- e-business

- payment processing technologies

- communication methods and efficiency

- intranets.

3) The impact of technology on employment

As an aspiring P&D specialist you need to pay particular attention to the consequences of technological advances for the world of employment and labour markets. You might like to consider the following:

- need for new skills

- skills obsolescence

- de-skilling

- training and development needs

- e-recruitment

- personnel databases

- productivity improvements and redundancies

- health and safety implications

- confidentiality and surveillance issues

- organisational structure

- teleworking.

4) The impact of technology on society

Finally, it is necessary to consider the wider impact of new technologies on society in general. Here it is possible to identify many negative as well as positive developments. Fierce debates rage about some innovations such as genetically modified foods and cloning. Try to develop some understanding of these issues. Areas to consider are the following:

- uncertainty and insecurity

- pollution and depletion of natural resources

- global warming

- suspicion of technological developments

- medical advances

- fuelling consumerism

- educational improvements

- time-saving technologies

- widening human horizons.

Sources of information

There is no single source of information about the technological environment currently included on the CIPD's library holding list. However, all the textbooks that cover the business context in general terms include extensive chapters on the subject. The emphasis differs, but between them all the above topics are well covered. You will find it useful to read Farnham (Chapter 6), Brooks & Weatherston (Chapters 4 & 6), Morris et al (Chapter 6), Palmer & Hartley (Chapter 12) and Cartwright (Chapter 7). There is also an excellent chapter on current technological developments and their significance for business organisations in Peter Dicken's *Global Shift* (2003). In addition, there is regular coverage of major technological developments in *The Economist* each week and in their annual publication looking forward to the coming year (*The World in 2003, 2004* etc). This is published in November each year and is well worth reading in preparation for the Managing in a Business Context exam.

International factors

1) Globalisation and international trade

Debates about the desirability and impact of globalisation are central to an understanding of the contemporary business context. Questions on such matters thus feature regularly on Managing in a Business Context exam papers. You will find it helpful to familiarise yourself with the following:

- evolving patterns of international trade

- causes of globalisation

- debates about the significance of globalisation

- arguments in favour of globalisation

- sceptical views on globalisation

- impact of globalisation on different countries

- impact of globalisation on UK organisations

- impact of globalisation on UK employees and employment markets.

2) International institutions

The Standards make specific mention of various international institutions that have responsibility for economic development and finance at a global level. You therefore need to be familiar with the role and function played by each and, if possible, have developed views about the way they operate. A knowledge of some of the critiques of their activities always impresses examiners. The institutions concerned are as follows:

- General Agreement on Tariffs and Trade (GATT)

- the International Labour Organization (ILO)

- the International Monetary Fund (IMF)

- the Organization for Economic Co-operation and Development (OECD)

- the World Bank (WB)

- the World Trade Organisation (WTO).

3) Regional groupings

The other major international institutions of consequence in determining the business context are regional rather than global. While the emphasis must inevitably be on the European Union, you are also expected to know broadly what other groupings exist and how they operate in practice. Here is a list of topic areas to help you plan your revision:

- the reasons for the rise of regional economic groupings

- the size and scope of EU activity

- debates about the future development of the EU (ie: political union/expansion etc)

- debates about Britain's future role in the EU

- the Asian Free Trade Area (AFTA)/Association of South East Asian Nations (ASEAN)

- the North American Free Trade Agreement (NAFTA)

- other common markets (eg: CARICOM, EFTA and MERCOSUR).

4) Transnational/multinational companies

Finally, you also need to be in a position to write about the particular issues facing multinational organisations and some of the wider debates about their growth and influence:

- the key characteristics of a transnational/multinational corporation

- the reasons for their growth in recent decades

- sources of competitive advantage

- arguments for and against the continued growth of TNCs

- P&D issues particular to TNCs/MNCs

- interactions between government and TNCs/MNCs.

Sources of information

There are two books included on CIPD library holding lists that deal specifically with the international business context. *Global Shift* by Peter Dicken, a new edition of which came out in 2003, is a superb introduction to all the debates in this field. It goes into far greater detail than is needed for the purposes of the CIPD examination, but is a very good starting point. The textbook by Harrison et al (2000) takes a more European focus and covers all the topic areas listed above. You will also find plenty of relevant material in McCormick's (2002) book on the European Union. Treatment in the general texts on the business environment is varied. The relevant chapters are Farnham (Chapter 7), Palmer & Hartley (Chapter 10) and Brooks & Weatherston (Chapter 3). The others infuse each of their other chapters with international examples, but do not give the subject specific coverage. Here too, as with the other subjects, you need to try to keep up to date with unfolding developments and debates – particularly on the European Union.

Social responsibility and ethics

1) Ethics and organisational stakeholders

Issues relating to business ethics appear in various forms on Managing in a Business Context exam papers. Sometimes questions are asked about the subject in general terms, but more often they ask you to reflect on practice in your own organisations. A third type of question relates ethics to other issues covered in the Standards. Stakeholder perspectives provide a useful framework for thinking about business ethics. You should consider the following topics:

- links between stakeholder theory and business ethics

- internal and external stakeholders

- the objectives of different stakeholders

- conflict between different stakeholder interests

- influence of different stakeholders

- stakeholders in the public and voluntary sectors.

2) Accountability

The major way in which society seeks to ensure a high level of ethical practice in organisations is by making them accountable for their actions in various ways. These systems of accountability are by no means perfect, but they play a very influential role. You need to be familiar with the principal approaches used in the UK and their relative effectiveness in practice:

- accountability to shareholders

- legal accountability vis a vis other stakeholders

- corporate reputation and the media

- political accountability (eg public sector and privatised utilities)

- accountability to trade organisations and professional bodies.

3) Social responsibility

Debates about corporate social responsibility have become increasingly prominent in recent years, following the uncovering of various scandals and examples of malpractice. Debates also rage about the ethics of some established business practices and the sale of goods such as tobacco. You need to be in a position to give some examples of these and to be able to define social responsibility both in general terms and from the perspective of your own organisation. The following headings should help you to organise your thinking:

- major ethical dilemmas faced by organisations

- debates about definitions of business ethicality

- duties of organisations

- cases for and against high levels of ethical practice from a business perspective

- written policies and statements on ethics

- ethics in the public sector.

4) Professionalism

The concept of professionalism also plays a major part in thinking about business ethics and has a particular significance for you sitting exams for membership of a professional body. You thus need to be familiar with the activities of such bodies and the way that they seek to maintain high ethical standards. You may like to organise your revision around the following five broad themes:

- defining professional conduct

- the role of professional bodies

- types of professional control

- codes of conduct

- professional issues for HR practitioners.

Sources of information

Not all standard textbooks on the business environment cover ethics and professionalism as discrete topics, although most make reference to ethical issues when discussing other core subject areas. You will find Farnham (Chapter 8) to be a good starting point. Palmer & Hartley (Chapter 5) and Morris et al (Chapter 2) also provide introductions. Campbell et al (Chapter 14) is particularly strong on stakeholder perspectives and social responsibility. *Managing Business Ethics* by Trevino and Nelson (2003) is good at presenting ethical dilemmas and assessing management actions in a very practical way. There are also many other texts available that are strong on the theoretical perspectives. In many ways the best approach to take in preparing yourself for exam questions in this area is to reflect on your own experience and that of organisations you have worked in.

INDEX

NOTES